GAME DAY
ARIZONA STATE FOOTBALL

Derek Hagan

GAME DAY
ARIZONA STATE FOOTBALL

The Greatest Games, Players, Coaches and Teams
in the Glorious Tradition of Sun Devil Football

TRIUMPH
BOOKS

Athlon® Sports™
AMERICA'S PREMIER SPORTS ANNUALS

Library of Congress Control Number: 2007903111

This book is available in quantity at special discounts for your group or organization. For further information, contact:

Triumph Books
542 South Dearborn Street
Suite 750
Chicago, Illinois 60605
(312) 939-3330
Fax (312) 663-3557

CONTRIBUTING WRITER: Scott Bordow

EDITOR: Rob Doster

PHOTO EDITOR: Tim Clark
ASSISTANT PHOTO EDITOR: Danny Murphy

DESIGN: Eileen Wagner
PRODUCTION: Patricia Frey

PHOTO CREDITS: Athlon Sports Archive, AP/Wide World Photos, Joseph Healey, Arizona State University

Printed in China

ISBN: 978-1-60078-018-9

Contents

Foreword by Jeff Van Raaphorst.........................vii

Introduction xi

The Greatest Players..................................1

The Coaches....................................... 49

Sun Devil Superlatives......................... 61

The Rivalries.................................... 89

Talkin' Arizona State Football 109

Traditions and Pageantry 123

Facts and Figures 141

Jeff Van Raaphorst

Foreword

Arizona State followed a non-traditional approach to college football by playing evening games; while the players spent the day in a hotel anticipating kickoff, the fans finished daily activities and then donned their maroon and gold and made their way to the stadium between the buttes. The warm late summer and crisp fall evenings made the raucous crowd in Sun Devil Stadium the place to be on a Saturday evening in Phoenix. The momentum would build daily during the week as the local media would preview the upcoming opponent that would be invading our stadium. Arizona State football shared the local spotlight with the Phoenix Suns and enjoyed tremendous support. These are the memories that I have of playing in the greatest stadium in the Southwest on game night; they can be summarized in three words: passion, place and players.

The Sun Devil faithful were a very passionate and supportive component of the success that Frank Kush had established as the Sun Devils left the Western Athletic Conference and entered conference play in the Pac-10. As a Southern California recruit, I had observed the fickle fans in the Golden State that would base their attendance on one of their many weekend entertainment opportunities. That was not the case with our 12th man; they would consistently fill Sun Devil Stadium, making it challenging for opposing teams. The game day experience that I observed when I first entered the stadium as a high school senior was something that I had never observed in California, and I knew that I wanted to attend a university where football was king.

From a player's perspective Sun Devil Stadium was mesmerizing. When we emerged from our dressing room into the lights and cheers from the South end zone, you could feel the expectation that was present, the expectation to win. The fans were not in a large bowl like the Coliseum or the Rose Bowl; they were not separated from the field by a track. They were a part of the game and towered over the contest in their vertical confines. The grass was always perfectly manicured and cut short to allow for our fast style of play. Players will tell you that there is no better playing surface in the Pac-10 than at Sun Devil Stadium.

The players, my teammates, are what I personally will remember the most about the time that I spent at ASU. We came from all different parts of the country and were added to the desert recruits. We traveled north to Tontozona, our summer practice facility in the mountains. The time that we spent there was entirely focused on football and teamwork. Before a team can win a single game you must learn to become friends, how to trust each other, how to leave your past accomplishments behind and look ahead to a common goal of winning a Pac-10 championship. Other great Sun Devil teams started a legacy that we wanted to continue. When the 1986 team stood victorious in the Rose Bowl on January 1, 1987, I knew that I had been blessed with a great opportunity that I would never forget. I got to play with great friends, in a great stadium and in front of great crowds.

Thanks, ASU, for the opportunity, and Go Devils!

—Jeff Van Raaphorst

Introduction

The images are unforgettable and too numerous to count.

Jake Plummer, slithering through cracks in the defense and making countless big plays. Frank Kush, bringing unmatched intensity to Tempe and launching Arizona State football into the national consciousness. John Jefferson, stretching his body to make one of the greatest catches in college football history. Jeff Van Raaphorst, leading ASU to Rose Bowl glory. A program-defining win in the Fiesta Bowl over highly regarded Nebraska. A packed Sun Devil Stadium, giving full-throated support to the beloved Sun Devils. Championships won; legends created.

We're distilling the pageantry and drama of Arizona State football into the pages that follow. It's a daunting task. Few college football programs in the country inspire the loyalty and passion that the Sun Devil football program exacts from its fans—and with good reason.

The numbers alone are impressive: 12 bowl victories. Six former Sun Devils in the

College Football Hall of Fame. Countless statistical milestones.

But numbers alone don't do justice to the history of Arizona State football. The Sun Devil program stands for something deeper. Juan Roque, the great ASU offensive lineman, put it this way: "The best days of my life were when I was a student-athlete at ASU. Donning the Maroon and Gold on Saturdays and playing alongside my Sun Devil brothers was special and I take great pride in what we accomplished as a team and I cherish the relationships I have with my brothers to this day. Athletics is just part of the experience though. ASU is full of great people who do a great job in supporting student-athletes. Everyone I met on campus—whether it be professors, academic advisors, or the staff at the scholarship office—made my days as a college student great. The Athletic Department staff also provided tremendous support and always had the best interests of the athletes in mind. ASU is about family; once you're in, you're in for life!"

Through the words and images we present, you'll get a taste of what Arizona State football is all about. If you're a true Sun Devil fan, we can guarantee many proud moments—and a few chill bumps—by the time you're finished.

Pat Tillman

The Greatest Players

Arizona State is not considered a traditional college power along the lines of USC, Ohio State or Florida.

The Sun Devils haven't won a national championship. They've been to two Rose Bowls since joining the Pac-10 in 1978. Most years, they're relegated to second-tier bowl games.

But that seeming lack of success hasn't seemed to impact the number or quality of players who have held court at Sun Devil Stadium over the years.

As of 2006, ASU had sent 109 players to the NFL. At least one Sun Devil has played in 11 of the last 14 Super Bowls. ASU was one of only three schools in the country—Miami and Florida State were the others—to have a player taken in the first round of the NFL draft every year from 2000 to 2003.

If there's a common characteristic of ASU's great players, it's speed. Rarely are the Sun Devils able to recruit the best offensive or defensive linemen in the country. They pursue the athlete, the kid who can grow into his position or simply be quicker than the player lining up opposite him.

This isn't a complete list of ASU's great players. There are too many to count. But it is a fairly comprehensive highlight reel of some of the top names in school history.

PAT TILLMAN
Linebacker
5'11", 204 pounds
San Jose, California

Tillman was considered too small and too slow to play major college football. Only three Division I-A schools offered him a scholarship.

ASU didn't think Tillman would be anything special. A special teams player. A backup. A good character guy who would help the team win and be a positive influence in the locker room.

But as we know now, Tillman's whole life was about defying expectations. It's why he turned down a $9 million contract offer from the St. Louis Rams to stay with the Arizona Cardinals, the team that drafted him.

It's why, in the wake of the 9/11 terrorist attacks, he left the NFL behind to enlist in the U.S. Army. In April of 2004, Cpl. Pat Tillman was killed in the line of duty in Afghanistan.

By then, Tillman was a larger-than-life figure, a man who embodied virtue and courage and integrity.

Too often, the word "hero" is tossed about in sports as if it were meant to describe athletic exploits. Tillman was a hero in the truest sense of the word.

The first clue that Tillman wasn't your typical college football player came in 1994, when then-ASU coach Bruce Snyder asked him about redshirting. "Dude," Tillman said, "I'm not planning on staying that long. I've got things to do."

Tillman wasn't an instant success at ASU. He didn't start a game his freshman year and started only one his sophomore season.

But in 1996, he burst onto the national scene. Getting a chance to start at linebacker, he had 91 tackles, four interceptions and two quarterback sacks. He was named second-team All-Pac-10.

As a senior in 1997, Tillman led ASU in tackles with 97 and was named the Pac-10 Defensive Player of the Year. He also was named second-team All-American by the Associated Press and was an Academic All-American for his 3.82 grade point average in marketing.

With his long hair flowing out of the back of his helmet and his unique lifestyle—he would climb up the light towers at Sun Devil Stadium to think—Tillman became one of the most popular players ever to wear maroon and gold.

But it wasn't just the way he played that captured hearts. It was the way he lived.

Tillman was adored by females on campus, yet he never cheated on his sweetheart, Marie, who would later become his wife.

He could have had a huge ego, but he was more interested in learning about others than he was bragging about himself.

The playbook was the least interesting thing he read.

"He'd come to my office at 10 or 11 PM every night," said then-ASU linebackers coach Lyle Setencich. "We'd sit down and talk about God or Kosovo or poor people in this country. He wanted me to read the Book of Mormon. So we did."

PAT TILLMAN
AT A GLANCE

- 1994: 10 tackles, one sack
- 1995: 47 tackles, one sack
- 1996: 91 tackles, two sacks, four interceptions
- 1997: 93 tackles, four sacks, three interceptions
- Pac-10 Defensive Player of the Year in 1997
- Second-team All-American (Associated Press) in 1997
- Instrumental part of ASU's 11–1 1996 Rose Bowl team

Rugged, intense, individualistic and ultimately heroic—Pat Tillman was one of a kind.

Although the 1996 ASU Rose Bowl team was filled with great players—Jake Plummer, Keith Poole, Juan Roque, Derrick Rodgers, etc.—it was Tillman who became the team's emotional leader.

"You don't find guys that have that combination of being as bright and as tough as him," said Phil Snow, ASU's defensive coordinator at the time. "This guy could go live in a foxhole for a year by himself with no food."

The night before ASU's game against No. 1 Nebraska in September of 1996, a players-only meeting was held at the team hotel. It was Tillman who set the mood.

"That was the first time I saw Pat speak out," wide receiver Ricky Boyer said. "I think we broke a greaseboard and some chairs."

ASU beat Nebraska, 19–0, setting the stage for an 11–0 regular season and a trip to the Rose Bowl, where it lost to Ohio State.

Tillman's death in 2004 hit the ASU community hard. Although everyone knew that war didn't discriminate, Tillman seemed indestructible.

"We lost a truly great young man; very simply, the ultimate American," said Kevin White, ASU's athletic director from 1996 to 2000. "To me, Pat Tillman is, without question, the biggest hero of my lifetime.

"During my tenure at ASU, Pat was often referred to by many of us as 'Braveheart.' How incredibly ironic, years later, that Pat will go down in the annals of American history as the quintessential, in every way, braveheart."

The Quarterbacks

Penn State is known as "Linebacker U." USC is where great tailbacks go to run. Arizona State has no such distinction among fans in other parts of the country, but over the years it has produced a steady diet of terrific college quarterbacks.

The first in a long line of signal-callers was Joe Spagnola, better known in Tempe as "Spaghetti Joe."

Spagnola wasn't particularly fast or particularly big, and he didn't have the greatest throwing arm. All he did was win.

Coach Frank Kush made him the starter as a sophomore in 1968, and over the next three years the Devils went 27–4, capped by an 11–0 season and a 48–26 Peach Bowl victory over North Carolina in 1970.

Spagnola's statistics weren't awe-inspiring. He threw nearly as many interceptions (28) as touchdowns (35) in his career, but at the end of the day his teams won—and lit up the scoreboard.

ASU averaged 38.8 points and 463 total yards per game during Spagnola's tenure.

Any thought that the program might suffer upon Spagnola's departure was unfounded, because Kush had another ready-made winner waiting in the wings.

A guy by the name of Danny White.

White was a legacy at ASU, the son of famed halfback Wilford "Whizzer" White. But he wasn't a big-time recruit for the Sun Devils. In fact, Kush had no football scholarships left, so he convinced baseball coach Bobby Winkles to give White a baseball scholarship.

Kush never could thank Winkles enough.

White was the starting quarterback for three of the greatest teams in ASU history. The 1971 squad went 11–1 and beat Florida State in the Fiesta Bowl; the 1972 team finished 10–2 and beat Missouri in the Fiesta Bowl; and the 1973 club ended the year 11–1 with a victory over Pittsburgh in the Fiesta Bowl.

That's a 32–4 record and three straight bowl wins.

White learned early on that Kush wouldn't afford him special status because he was Whizzer White's son.

During spring practice following White's freshman season, he threw a pass to the tight end that hit the ground in front of him. Kush

College Hall of Famer Danny White

walked over and slapped White on the helmet and said, "You weak-armed (expletive-deleted). I ought to fire the coach who recruited you."

Said White: "He didn't hurt me, but he shocked me and after the shock wore away, anger kind of set in. I became determined to prove to him that he was wrong about me."

The Sun Devils were so talented during White's tenure they likely would have measured up to college football's powerhouses. White, though, was anything but a caretaker of the offense.

He made several All-America teams as a senior and finished his career with 64 touchdown passes and 6,717 yards passing. By comparison, Jake Plummer, considered one of the elite players in ASU history, started four seasons and threw 65 TD passes.

White was not just a pretty face and a golden arm. He was as tough as he was talented. Before a game against New Mexico he could barely lift his right arm above his head because of a shoulder injury.

Kush's advice?

"Give it to someone who knows what to do with it."

White threw six touchdown passes.

In 1998, he became the first Sun Devil player to be elected into the College Football Hall of Fame. *Sports Illustrated* named him the second-best college quarterback of all time, behind BYU's Steve Young.

He would go on to great success in the NFL as the quarterback for the Dallas Cowboys. Later, he became a championship coach in the Arena Football League for the Arizona Rattlers.

White long was considered the standard-bearer for ASU quarterbacks. He was followed by a long line of Sun Devils who had good numbers and successful seasons.

That list wouldn't be complete without a mention of Mark Malone. The Tom Selleck look-alike played just two seasons (1978–1979) at ASU, but in those two years he threw for 24 touchdowns and 3,459 yards. Malone had his greatest success in the NFL, however. A first-round pick of the Pittsburgh Steelers in 1979, he played eight seasons in the Steel City before finishing his career with the San Diego Chargers and New York Jets. He wound up fourth on Pittsburgh's all-time passing list with 8,582 yards passing. Malone will always be remembered fondly in Arizona State lore for

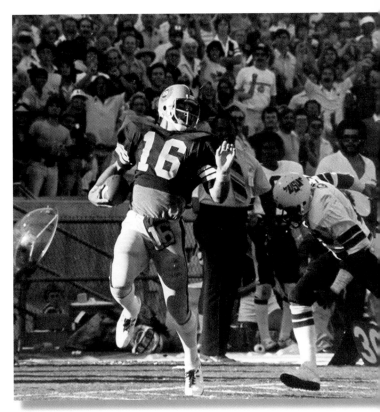

Mark Malone made his mark in only two seasons in Tempe.

leading the Sun Devils' stunning 20–7 upset of powerhouse Southern California in 1978.

But even with Malone's success, it seemed that no one could match the legacy that White had left. That is, until Jeff Van Raaphorst did exactly that.

The southern California recruit started three years at ASU. His first two seasons (1984–1985) were largely forgettable as the Sun Devils went 5–6 and 8–4.

But in 1986 Van Raaphorst did something only one other Sun Devil quarterback has accomplished. He led ASU to the Rose Bowl. And he also did something no other Sun Devil signal-caller has done; he led his team to a win once they got there.

The Sun Devils finished 10–1–1 and beat Michigan, 22–15, in the Rose Bowl. The Devils trailed, 8–0, after the first quarter, but Van Raaphorst brought ASU back, completing two touchdown passes to flanker Bruce Hill. He was named the game's Most Valuable Player after completing 16-of-30 passes for 193 yards and two touchdowns, with no interceptions.

"In the locker room before the game, I dropped my radio, and Coach (John) Cooper dropped his Coke," Van Raaphorst said. "We both looked at each other and laughed and said, 'Hey, that better not happen in the game.'"

The victory was particularly sweet for Van Raaphorst because in 1961 his father, Dick, a kicker at Ohio State, was denied a chance to play in the game after the school faculty voted to prohibit the Buckeyes from participating because it thought football was being overemphasized.

"It's a dream come true," Van Raaphorst said. "My father never got a chance to do it, and I'm just glad I was able to. This is for him."

Van Raaphorst continues to maintain a connection with ASU. He's a radio color commentator for Sun Devil broadcasts.

Ten years after Van Raaphorst created his Pasadena lagacy, a different kind of quarterback led ASU to the Rose Bowl.

Jake Plummer wasn't as cerebral as Van Raaphorst. He made mistakes that would drive the coaching staff crazy. But he had an indefatigable spirit and the ability to play his best when his team needed him most.

He also was a free spirit who endeared himself to teammates with his kookiness. He often danced the funky chicken in the locker room—naked.

Plummer started as a true freshman in 1993, and his statistics improved every season. But the Sun Devils struggled, going 6–5 in 1993, 3–8 in 1994 and 6–5 in 1995.

Like Van Raaphorst, however, Plummer had a special senior season. He threw for 2,776 yards and 24 touchdowns, with 10 interceptions. No game displayed more of his value to ASU than the Sun Devils' 42–34 victory over UCLA on October 12. Plummer threw for a touchdown, ran for a touchdown and caught a touchdown pass.

In the Sun Devils' 20–17 Rose Bowl loss to Ohio State, he scored what appeared to

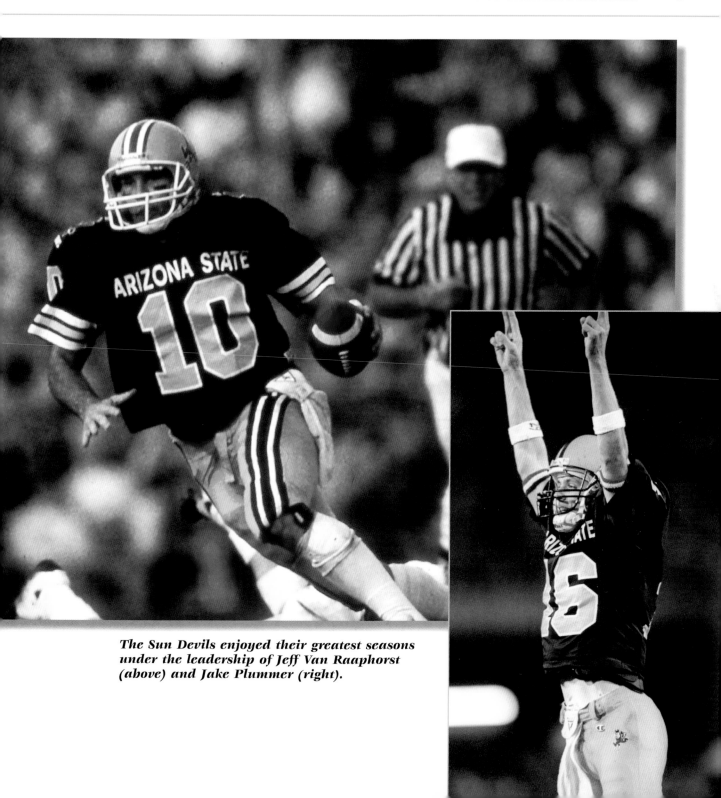

The Sun Devils enjoyed their greatest seasons under the leadership of Jeff Van Raaphorst (above) and Jake Plummer (right).

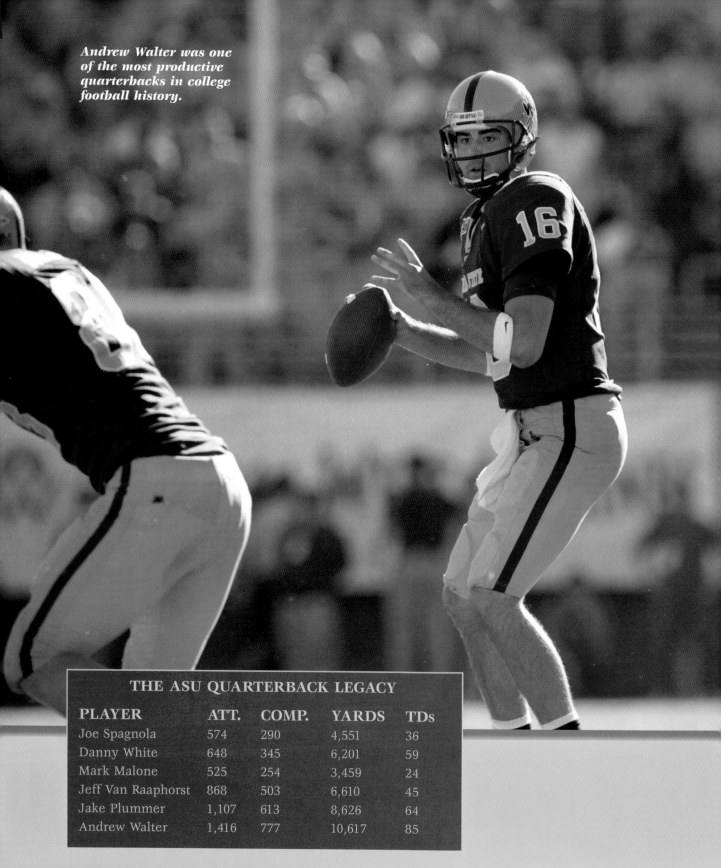

Andrew Walter was one of the most productive quarterbacks in college football history.

THE ASU QUARTERBACK LEGACY

PLAYER	ATT.	COMP.	YARDS	TDs
Joe Spagnola	574	290	4,551	36
Danny White	648	345	6,201	59
Mark Malone	525	254	3,459	24
Jeff Van Raaphorst	868	503	6,610	45
Jake Plummer	1,107	613	8,626	64
Andrew Walter	1,416	777	10,617	85

be the game-winning touchdown with 100 seconds left only to see the Buckeyes go down the field and score.

"There is not a single player in college football who means more to his team than Jake Plummer," coach Bruce Snyder said. "We all should just be enjoying this guy. He's a heck of a football player. He is one of the best young players I have ever been around. If I were starting a team from scratch, he would be my first pick."

Plummer made several All-America teams and finished third in the Heisman Trophy voting his senior season. He was a second-round draft choice by the Arizona Cardinals in 1997 and a year later led the Cardinals to their first playoff win in 51 years.

Andrew Walter, who started from 2001 to 2004, didn't have the success Van Raaphorst and Plummer had. But no quarterback in school history put up the numbers he did.

Walter was fortunate to play in coach Dirk Koetter's pass-first system. But a quarterback still has to make the throws, and Walter could make every one of them. Few quarterbacks in college football history, it could be argued, threw the deep ball better than Walter.

He finished his career as ASU's all-time leader in passing attempts (1,416), completions (777), touchdown passes (85) and passing yards (10,617). He became the Pac-10's all-time leader in touchdown passes, eclipsing the mark set by Stanford legend John Elway.

Walter was one of the few players who grew up knowing he would become a Sun Devil. His family owned a cabin near Camp Tontozona, the bucolic retreat where ASU holds its fall practices, and Walter would attend ASU's workouts as a kid.

He became the starter midway through his freshman year, replacing Chad Christensen, and never looked back.

Spagnola, White, Malone, Van Raaphorst, Plummer and Walter. Pretty good for a university not known to be "Quarterback U."

THEY CAN RUN, TOO

ASU didn't simply throw the ball with great success over the years. It's produced a long list of quality running backs, starting with a famous name in 1950 and most recently with a not-so-famous name in 2006.

The Sun Devils were a non-descript, struggling program when Wilford "Whizzer" White arrived on campus in 1947. ASU had gone 2–7–2 the year before and lost to archrival Arizona, 67–0.

That loss, ironically, led White to ASU. He was at the game and thought the Wildcats left their starters in too long and ran up the score.

His disdain for UA left ASU battling Tennessee for his name on a letter-of-intent. In Bob Eger's book, *Maroon and Gold, A History of Sun Devil Athletics*, White said Tennessee offered him inducements to come to Knoxville, including a car.

But White, a Mesa High product, wanted to play closer to home. He signed with ASU and forever changed the face of Sun Devil football.

ASU's record improved every year White played, from 4–7 in 1947 to 9–2 in 1950. As a senior, White rushed for 1,502 yards and 22 touchdowns. His nickname was "the Brain," because he so easily picked up coach Ed Doherty's innovative offensive schemes.

In his final regular-season game as a Sun Devil, White scored seven touchdowns against Idaho. He was taken out late in the game to a standing ovation from the home crowd.

"It was a great day, but a sad time," White told Eger. "They got a picture of me sitting on the bench boo-hooing at the end."

There's a terrific picture of Leon Burton in ASU's archives striking the Heisman Trophy pose. Burton didn't win the award, but he had a season for the ages in 1957, leading the nation in rushing (1,126 yards) and scoring (96 points). His 9.6 yards per carry set an NCAA record. He had 34 touchdowns in his college career.

What's astounding about Burton's production is that he wasn't even the featured back in ASU's offense. He shared the load with Bobby Mulgado in three of his four seasons.

Art Malone isn't as omnipresent in ASU's record books as White is. He had one stellar season for the Sun Devils. But what a season it was.

In 1968 Malone, who had been moved from halfback to fullback, rushed for 1,431 yards on 235 carries, a 6.1 average. He scored 17 touchdowns on the ground and twice ran for more than 200 yards. He was named the Western Athletic Conference Player of the Year and later played six seasons in the NFL. After retiring, Malone worked for the ASU athletic department for 22 years.

Two seasons after Malone's departure, Woody Green embarked on arguably the greatest three-year stretch any Sun Devil has ever produced.

Wilford White

Art Malone

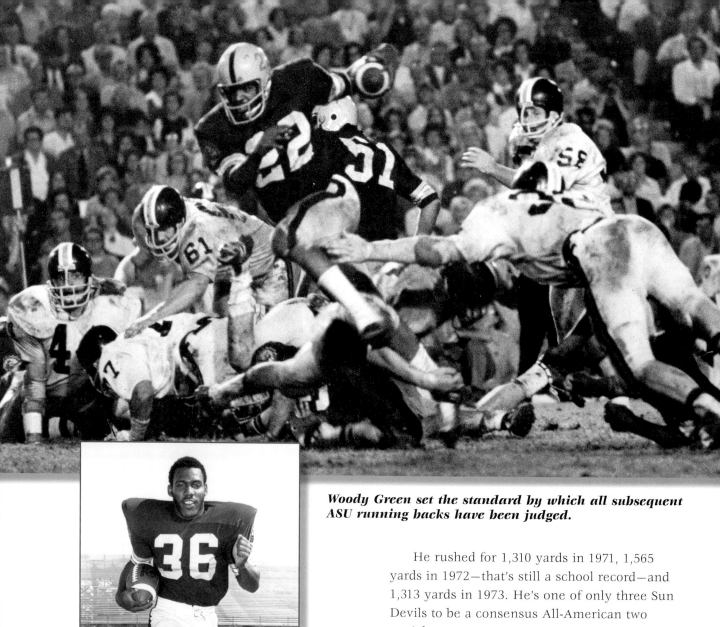

Freddie Williams

Woody Green set the standard by which all subsequent ASU running backs have been judged.

He rushed for 1,310 yards in 1971, 1,565 yards in 1972—that's still a school record—and 1,313 yards in 1973. He's one of only three Sun Devils to be a consensus All-American two straight years (1972, 1973).

Twenty-three years after he left school, Green remains ASU's all-time leader in rushing attempts (675), rushing yards (4,188) and rushing touchdowns (43).

ASU was churning out talented running backs in the 1970s, and Green gave way to "Fast" Freddie Williams.

Williams could fly, but he was also tough. He still leads all ASU backs in rushing attempts for a season, with 266. His 3,424

Darryl Clack

career yards rank second all-time to Green. Williams' best season came in 1975, when he rushed for 1,316 yards and ASU went 12–0.

Interestingly, most of ASU's best running backs played before 1980. ASU has had some good backs since then, but none of them have come close to equaling the output or having the impact of a Green, White or Malone.

Darryl Clack could have been that player, had injuries not interrupted his career. Few people would guess that Clack is the sixth-leading rusher in ASU history. But Clack, who had sprinter's speed, might be second on the list if a stress fracture of his right fibula hadn't limited him to 31 carries in 1985, his senior season. As it is, Clack rushed for 2,737 yards and 21 touchdowns in his career. His best season was 1984, when he ran for 1,052 yards and averaged 5.1 yards per carry.

Fullback Gerald Riggs never put up huge numbers at ASU because he shared the ball with tailbacks Robert Geathers and Willie Gittens. But ask Pac-10 defenders how tough Riggs was, and they'll have some war stories to tell. The 6'1", 225-pound Riggs bowled over defenders and in 1981 received All-Pac-10 honors after rushing for a team-high 891 yards. But it was in the NFL that Riggs truly made his mark.

Gerald Riggs

The ninth overall pick of the 1982 draft, he was named to three Pro Bowls. As an Atlanta Falcon, Riggs rushed for 1,719 yards and 10 touchdowns in 1985. Riggs was traded to Washington prior to the 1989 season, and two years later, he scored two touchdowns in Washington's 37–24 win over the Buffalo Bills in Super Bowl XXVI. He finished his career with 8,188 yards rushing and 69 touchdowns.

Perhaps the most talented back to come along in the past 20 years was California product J.R. Redmond. He ran for 3,299 yards between 1996 and 1999, ranking third in

J.R. Redmond

school history, and is second all-time in all-purpose yards with 5,617.

Redmond may be best remembered, however, for a pass he threw during the Rose Bowl season of 1996. His touchdown completion to Plummer helped ASU beat UCLA, 42–34, and remain undefeated at 6–0.

Ryan Torain won't play long enough to challenge ASU's career leaders in rushing.

But if his senior season is anything like his junior season, the tailback will be remembered as one of ASU's best junior college signings.

A powerful runner who also can make people miss, Torain rushed for 1,299 yards in 2006. If he has a similar season in 2007, he'll rank among ASU's career top-10 rushing leaders despite having played only two seasons.

THE 1,000-YARD SINGLE SEASON RUSHERS

Woody Green	1,565	1972
Wilford White	1,502	1950
Art Malone	1,431	1968
Freddie Williams	1,427	1975
Woody Green	1,313	1973
Woody Green	1,310	1971
Freddie Williams	1,299	1974
Ryan Torain	1,299	2006
Max Anderson	1,188	1967
Ben Malone	1,186	1973
J.R. Redmond	1,174	1999
Leon Burton	1,126	1957
Mario Bates	1,111	1993
Terry Battle	1,077	1996
Darryl Clack	1,052	1984
Darryl Harris	1,042	1986
Delvon Flowers	1,041	2001
Michael Martin	1,031	1997
Bob Thomas	1,024	1970

Ryan Torain

DANNY WHITE
Quarterback
1970–1973
Inducted 1998

See *The Quarterbacks*, page 6

MIKE HAYNES
Cornerback
1972–1975
Inducted 2001

There's little doubt as to who was the best cornerback in ASU history. Haynes was a two-time All-American and three-time All-Western Athletic Conference selection.

Haynes intercepted 17 passes in his ASU career, including a nation-high 11 his junior year.

Coach Frank Kush called Haynes "Luxury," because he didn't have to worry about the receiver Haynes covered.

Teams didn't throw Haynes's way much as a senior, but his lock-down defense was vital as the Sun Devils went 12–0 and beat Nebraska in the Fiesta Bowl.

Haynes also was a terrific kick returner, scoring twice on punt returns in 1975. He's the only Sun Devil to be inducted into both the College Football Hall of Fame and the NFL Hall of Fame.

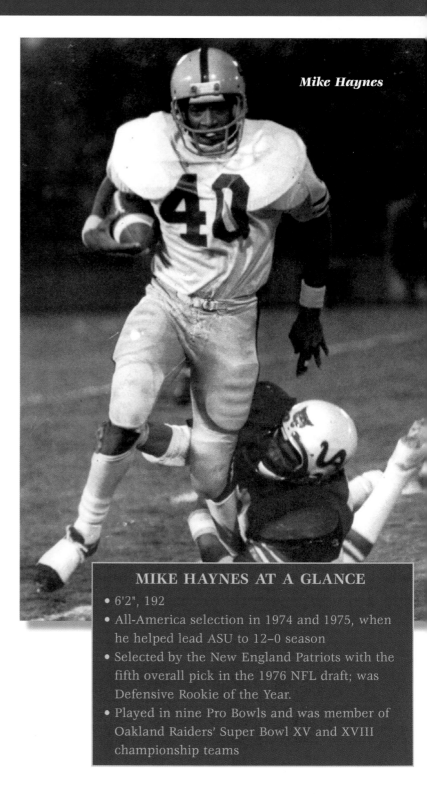

Mike Haynes

MIKE HAYNES AT A GLANCE
- 6'2", 192
- All-America selection in 1974 and 1975, when he helped lead ASU to 12–0 season
- Selected by the New England Patriots with the fifth overall pick in the 1976 NFL draft; was Defensive Rookie of the Year.
- Played in nine Pro Bowls and was member of Oakland Raiders' Super Bowl XV and XVIII championship teams

JOHN JEFFERSON AT A GLANCE

- 6'1", 198
- Two-time All-WAC selection and consensus All-American in 1977
- Selected by the San Diego Chargers in the first round of the 1978 NFL draft
- Played nine seasons in NFL, for Chargers, Green Bay Packers and Cleveland Browns; was first player in league history to gain 1,000 yards receiving in each of his first three seasons
- Led NFL in receiving yards in 1980 with 1,340

JOHN JEFFERSON
Wide Receiver
1974–1977
Inducted 2002

Jefferson will forever be remembered for "The Catch," considered the most memorable play in ASU history.

Against Arizona in the 1975 regular-season finale, with a Fiesta Bowl berth on the line, Jefferson laid out to catch a touchdown pass just before halftime to cut Arizona's lead to four points. ASU went on to win and beat Nebraska in the Fiesta Bowl to finish 12–0.

Jefferson's accomplishments, however, far exceeded that one game. He is ASU's all-time leader in receptions (188), yards (2,993) and consecutive games with a reception (44).

He was a consensus All-America selection in 1977, and was voted ASU's Most Valuable Player in 1975 and 1977.

*"**John had to be the epitome** of what college football was all about. He didn't have the greatest speed. He wasn't the biggest guy. He probably got the maximum out of what he had with concentration. He could run routes as well as anybody. The guy was remarkable—a class kid."*

—COACH FRANK KUSH

RON PRITCHARD
Linebacker
1966–1968
Inducted 2003

The Sun Devils weren't a household name in college football in the late 1960s, but Pritchard made everyone stand up and take notice. He was ASU's first consensus All-American after his senior season. Some long-time Sun Devil fans believe he was the best linebacker in school history.

RON PRITCHARD AT A GLANCE

- 6'1", 235
- ASU's first consensus All-American
- Three-time, first-team All-WAC selection
- Selected by the Houston Oilers in the first round of the 1969 NFL draft; played nine seasons with Oilers and Cincinnati Bengals

JUNIOR AH YOU
Defensive End
1969–1971

Ah You, a Hawaii native, was known as the "Hawaiian Punch" for his ability to drive quarterbacks into the ground. He was a three-time All-Western Athletic Conference selection, and he saved his best performances for the post season, being named the Outstanding Defensive Player of the Sun Devils' 1970 Peach Bowl win over North Carolina and their 1971 Fiesta Bowl victory over Florida State.

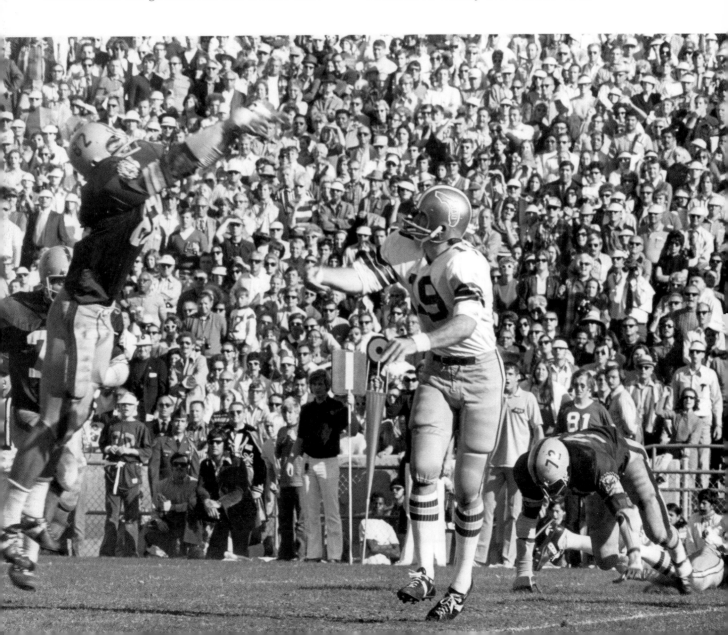

Eric Allen

Adam Archuleta

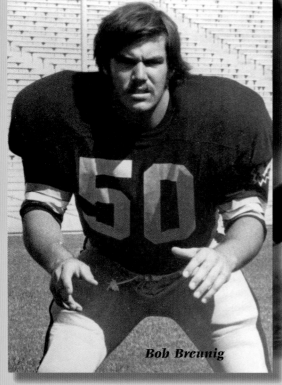

Bob Breunig

ERIC ALLEN
Cornerback
1984–1987

Don Shula called Eric Allen "one of the finest cornerbacks to ever play the game." He'll get no argument from Sun Devil fans, who watched Allen shut down receiver after receiver from 1984 to 1987. Allen wasn't the biggest defensive back at 5'10", nor was he the fastest, but he was a great technique player who never took a play off. He was an All-Pac-10 selection as a senior and a second-team All-American as chosen by the Associated Press. Allen went on to play 13 seasons in the NFL and make six Pro Bowl teams.

ADAM ARCHULETA
Linebacker
1997–2000

In the fall of 1997, an ASU publicist told a reporter that the skinny, acne-plagued Archuleta was the next Pat Tillman. The reporter laughed, knowing Archuleta was a walk-on from Chandler High School who had been ignored by most major colleges. In the end, however, Archuleta got the last laugh. He won a starting job as a sophomore and as a senior was named the Pac-10 Defensive Player of the Year for his 127 tackles, 15 tackles for loss, four sacks, four fumble recoveries, three forced fumbles and one interception.

BOB BREUNIG
Linebacker
1972–1974

Bruenig was a homegrown product out of Alhambra High School in Phoenix. He became a starter his sophomore season—collecting a team-high 91 tackles—and went on to have one of the most decorated careers in ASU history. As a senior, he made three All-America teams. Breunig was a third-round draft pick by the Dallas Cowboys in 1975 and had a long and productive NFL career.

Aaron Cox

CURLEY CULP
Nose Tackle
1965–1967

Culp was better known for his wrestling exploits at ASU. He was a national champion as a junior and went 45–0 in his final two years. But Culp also was a rock on the Sun Devils' defensive line. He was such an immovable force at his position that opponents were unable to run the ball up the middle. *The Sporting News* named Culp a first-team All-American in 1967. Culp's personality belied his competitive nature. The sports information staff never could get him to pose with a determined look on his face. He was always smiling.

Culp had a long and productive NFL career with the Chiefs, Oilers and Lions, making six appearances in the Pro Bowl.

AARON COX
Flanker
1984–1987

John Cooper likely would not have been the first coach in ASU history to lead the Sun Devils to the Rose Bowl without the contributions of flanker Aaron Cox. A three-year starter (1985–1987), Cox is fourth on ASU's all-time receiving list with 2,694 yards. He led the Sun Devils in receptions in each of the three years and earned All-Pac-10 honors in 1986 and 1987.

1985: 43 catches, 855 yards, 6 touchdowns
1986: 35 catches, 695 yards, 2 touchdowns
1987: 42 catches, 870 yards, 5 touchdowns

Curley Culp

DAVID FULCHER

Safety

1983–1985

Fulcher wasn't sold on the Sun
Devils from the beginning. In fact,
on national letter-of-intent day in
1982, both ASU and Arizona
claimed they had landed Fulcher.
The confusion was understandable;
Fulcher had told both UA assistant
Willie Peete and ASU aide Willie
Shaw that he was coming to their
schools. Fulcher, who at 6'3" and
228 pounds was bigger than many
of the linebackers in front of him,
signed with the Sun Devils and
became one of the best defenders in
school history. He had 110 tackles
as a freshman and was a consensus
All-American his sophomore and
junior seasons. He likely would
have made it a three-peat, but he
bypassed his senior year to enter
the NFL draft, where he was a third-
round choice of the Cincinnati
Bengals.

David Fulcher

DEREK HAGAN
Wide Receiver
2002–2005

Derek Hagan wasn't the fastest receiver ever to play for ASU. Nor was he the biggest. But few wideouts were better at doing the one thing they're supposed to do—catch the ball. Hagan's numbers are a bit inflated because he operated in Dirk Koetter's air strike offense, but there he is in the record books, first in career receptions (258) and career receiving yards (3,939). Hagan earned third-team All-America honors in 2005, his senior season, and All-Pac-10 honors as well.

2002: 32 catches, 405 yards, 0 touchdowns
2003: 66 catches, 1076 yards, 9 touchdowns
2004: 83 catches, 1,248 yards, 10 touchdowns
2005: 77 catches, 1,210 yards, 8 touchdowns

AL HARRIS
Defensive End
1975–1978

Harris will always hold a position of primacy for ASU as the first player to be a unanimous All-America selection. Harris earned that distinction after a 1978 season in which he had 46 unassisted tackles, 19 quarterback sacks and six pass deflections. The Chicago Bears drafted Harris with the ninth overall pick of the 1979 NFL draft. Harris was inducted into the ASU Sports Hall of Fame just three years after leaving school.

JOHN HARRIS
Safety
1975–1977

John Harris was the first in a long line of great safeties at Arizona State. He was first-team All-Western Athletic Conference in 1976 and 1977 and honorable mention Associated Press All-American both years. But Harris did more for ASU than just patrol the defensive backfield. He averaged in double digits in punt return yardage in 1976 and 1977. In addition, he was named the 1977 Sun Angel Male Athlete of the Year, honoring academic and athletic excellence.

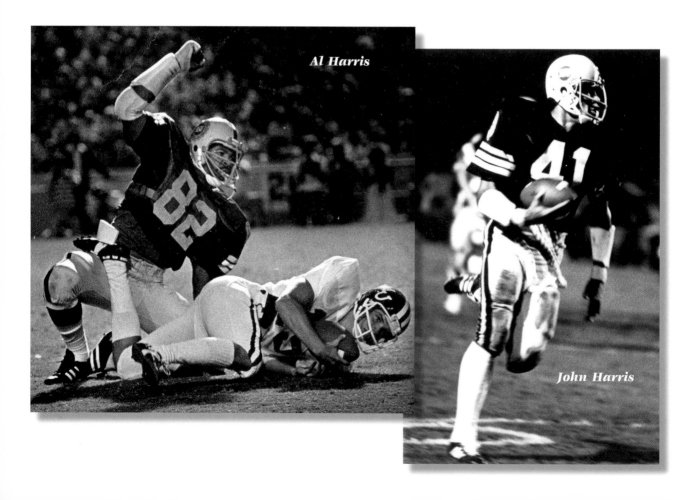

Al Harris

John Harris

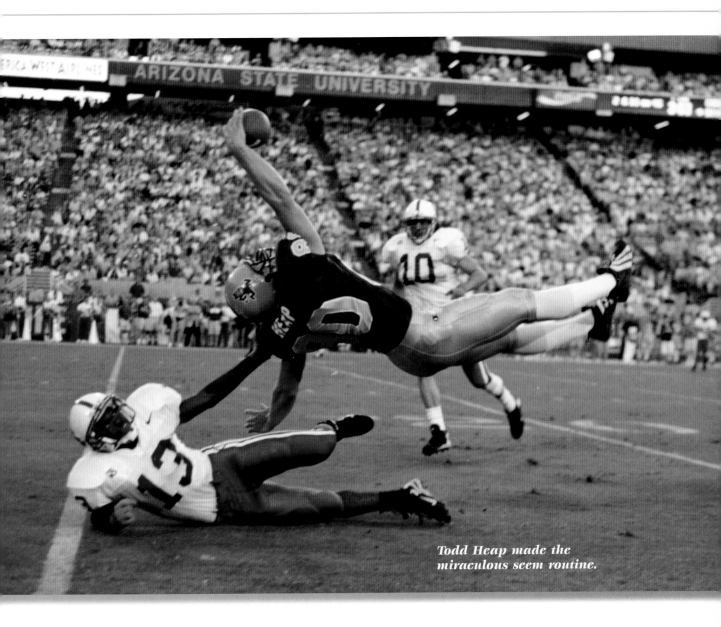

Todd Heap made the miraculous seem routine.

TODD HEAP
Tight End
1998–2000

Coach Bruce Snyder called Todd Heap the "Golden Retriever," because of his amazing ability to make one-handed catches in traffic, a talent he would show off in the NFL with the Baltimore Ravens. Heap, a local product from Mesa Mountain View High School, was All-Pac-10 both his junior and senior seasons.

1998: 12 catches, 209 yards, 4 touchdowns
1999: 55 catches, 832 yards, 3 touchdowns
2000: 48 catches, 644 yards, 3 touchdowns

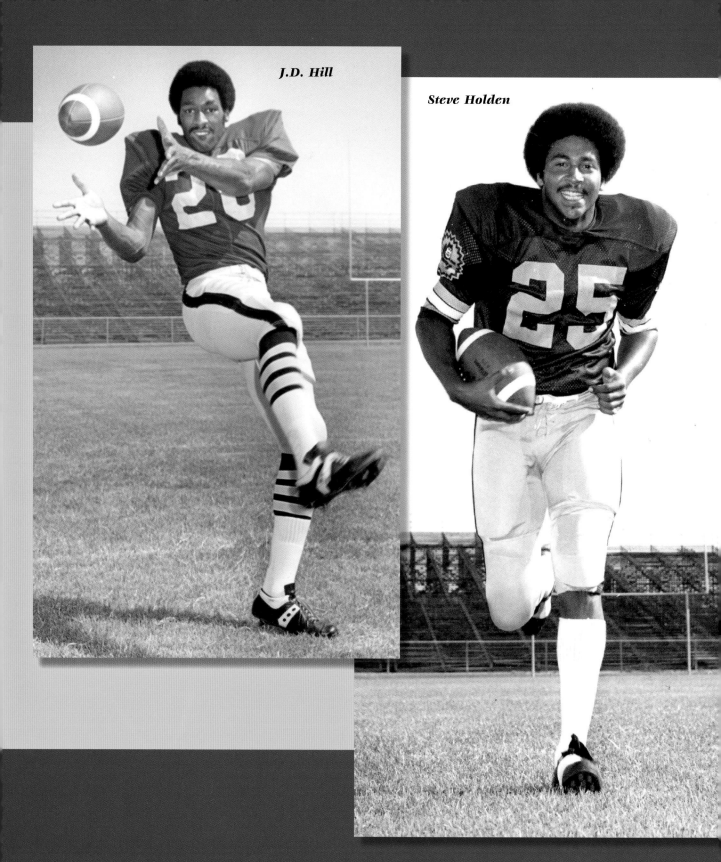

J.D. Hill

Steve Holden

J.D. HILL
Wide Receiver
1967–1968, 1970

Hill's career was interrupted in 1969 when he sat out the season because he was in coach Frank Kush's doghouse. But when he came back in 1970, he quickly made up for the time he lost. His 61 catches, 1,009 yards and 11 touchdowns that season were all school records. He was named first-team All-American by *The Sporting News*. Hill also was a track star, and in the 1968 WAC championships, he ran the 100-yard dash in 9.3 seconds—with sweats on.

1967: 34 catches, 587 yards, 8 touchdowns
1968: 23 catches, 391 yards, 3 touchdowns
1970: 61 catches, 1,009 yards, 11 touchdowns

STEVE HOLDEN
Wide Receiver
1970–1972

Steve Holden was part of the great Sun Devil teams in the early 1970s. A three-time All-Western Athletic Conference choice at wingback, Holden set five receiving records and led the nation in punt returns in 1970. How good was Holden? Those clubs had Danny White at quarterback and Woody Green at running back, and Holden was still named the Sun Devils' most valuable player for both the 1971 and 1972 seasons.

1970: 14 catches, 181 yards, 1 touchdown
1971: 38 catches, 848 yards, 12 touchdowns
1972: 42 catches, 911 yards, 12 touchdowns

JIM JEFFCOAT
Defensive End
1979–1982

It's impossible to name ASU's five greatest defensive linemen without having Jim Jeffcoat on the list. He had 20 career sacks. In his senior year, he collected 95 tackles, four sacks, four pass deflections and two forced fumbles. Those numbers helped ASU's defense rank first nationally in total defense (228.9 yards per game). Jeffcoat earned All-Pac-10 honors that season and the following April was a first-round draft choice of the Dallas Cowboys. He was a member of Dallas' 1983 and 1994 championship teams.

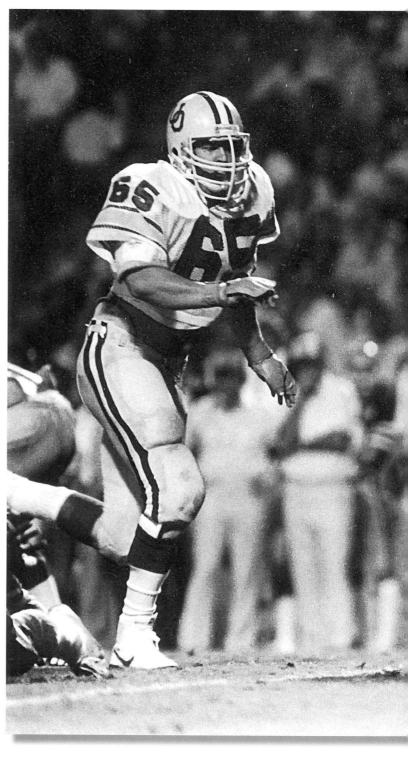

Jim Jeffcoat took his relentless style of play to the NFL, where he had an outstanding career with the Cowboys.

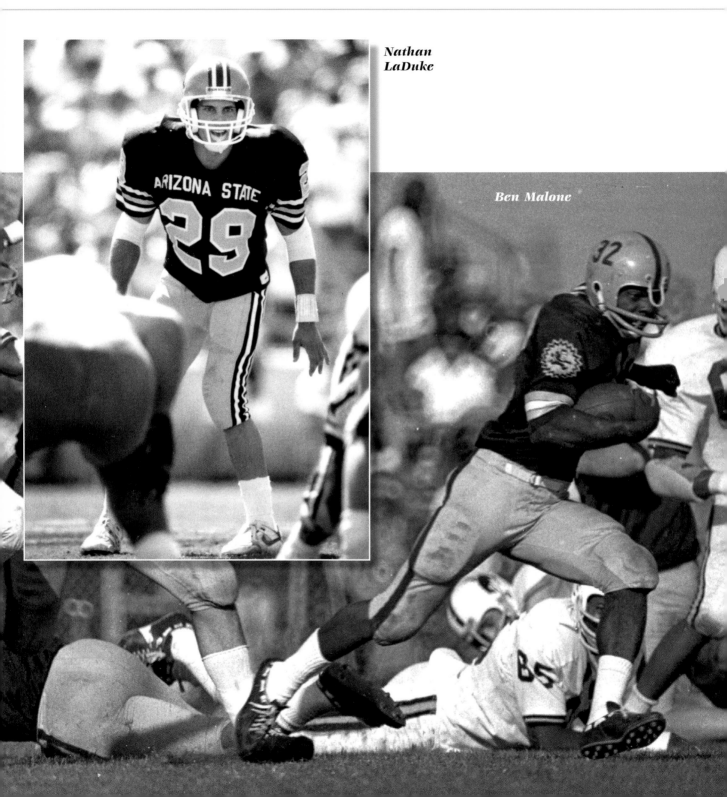

Nathan LaDuke

Ben Malone

NATHAN LaDUKE

Safety

1987–1990

Standing just 5'9" and lacking the speed usually needed to play free safety, Nathan LaDuke should have been just a bit player for ASU. But there were few Sun Devils who had a better feel for the game. LaDuke was both a terrific pass defender—he led ASU in interceptions in 1989 (six) and 1990 (four) and tied for the team lead in 1988 (three)—and a force along the line of scrimmage. He had 238 career solo tackles, tying linebacker Brett Wallerstedt for first place in that category. LaDuke earned second-team All-America honors in 1990 from the Associated Press, *The Sporting News* and *Football News*.

BEN MALONE

Running Back

1971–1973

Malone walked into a large shadow when he stepped foot onto the ASU campus. His older brother, Art, starred in the Sun Devil backfield in the late 1960s. It didn't take long, however, for Ben Malone to mark his own territory. In addition to opening holes for Woody Green, he averaged 6.4 yards per carry in his career, and on October 27, 1973, he had a game for the ages, rushing for 250 yards in a 44–14 victory over Oregon State. That season, Malone was part of the first backfield in ASU history to have all four members account for 1,000 yards; Green rushed for 1,313, quarterback Danny White threw for 2,878 yards and wingback Morris Owens had 1,076 receiving yards.

> 1971: 121 attempts, 917 yards, 4 touchdowns
> 1972: 73 attempts, 371 yards, 6 touchdowns
> 1973: 191 attempts, 1,186 yards, 15 touchdowns

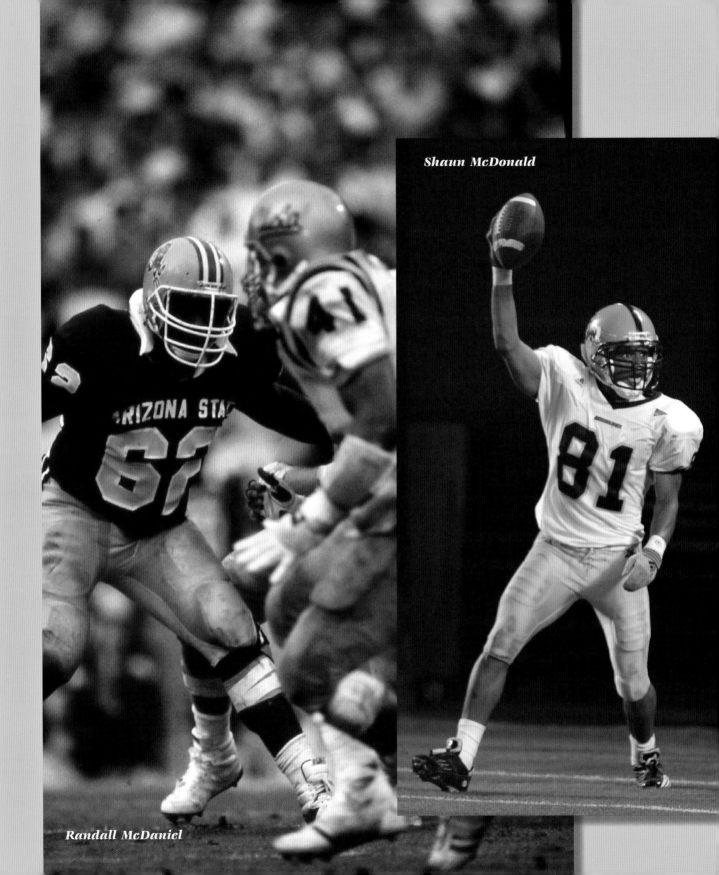

Shaun McDonald

Randall McDaniel

RANDALL McDANIEL

Guard

1984–1987

McDaniel was recruited as a tight end, but during the bye week of the 1984 season, coach Darryl Rogers moved him to guard and a star was born. McDaniel became one of only three ASU offensive lineman, along with Danny Villa and Juan Roque, to earn consensus All-America honors. His NFL career was even better. A first-round draft choice of the Minnesota Vikings in 1988, he played in 12 Pro Bowls, which remains a record. During the 2006 season, McDaniel was inducted into the Vikings' Ring of Honor.

SHAUN McDONALD

Wide Receiver

2000–2002

Dirk Koetter became ASU's coach in 2001, and no one benefited more from his arrival than diminutive wide receiver Shaun McDonald. The 5'10", 180-pound McDonald, a Phoenix native, became quarterback Andrew Walter's favorite target down the field, and his numbers are evidence of that. He made 47 catches for 1,104 yards and 10 touchdowns in 2001 then outdid himself the following year, grabbing 87 balls for 1,405 yards and 13 TDs. The 1,405 yards remain a school record.

> 2000: 22 catches, 358 yards, 1 touchdown
> 2001: 47 catches, 1,104 yards, 10 touchdowns
> 2002: 87 catches, 1,405 yards, 13 touchdowns

ZACH MILLER
Tight End
2003–2006

Most schools are fortunate to have one superb tight end every 10 years. ASU had two in a span of eight seasons. Miller, a local product from Desert Vista High School, lived up to his billing as Heap's heir apparent. He was a consensus All-American as a freshman and, like Heap, had a catchy nickname: "The Truth."

2004: 56 catches, 552 yards, 6 touchdowns
2005: 38 catches, 476 yards, 4 touchdowns
2006: 50 catches, 484 yards, 4 touchdowns

JOHN MISTLER
Wide Receiver
1978–1980

The 1979 season was the most tumultuous in ASU history. Legendary coach Frank Kush was fired after five games, and the Sun Devils finished 6–6, only their second non-winning season in 13 years. But wide receiver John Mistler didn't let the controversy over Kush's dismissal affect his game. He led ASU in receiving with 498 yards and four touchdowns, then followed that up with 53 catches for 573 yards and a touchdown as a senior. Mistler played six seasons in the NFL for the New York Giants and Buffalo Bills.

1977: 4 catches, 52 yards, 0 touchdowns
1978: 20 catches, 310 yards, 6 touchdowns
1979: 36 catches, 498 yards, 4 touchdowns
1980: 53 catches, 573 yards, 1 touchdowns

Zach Miller

John Mistler

KEITH POOLE
Wide Receiver
1993–1996

Poole wasn't the biggest receiver. Or the quickest. But he was as dependable as sunrise and sunset. Poole's velcro hands were vital for quarterback Jake Plummer during ASU's 1996 Rose Bowl season. Whenever Plummer needed a critical first down, he seemed to find Poole open between two defenders. Poole's personal story became well-known during his four years at ASU. His older brother, Marc, was a quadri-plegic. The brothers lived four miles away from each other but were rarely apart. Marc was a recognizable sight at every Sun Devil home game, waving his arms as he sat in a wheelchair on the sideline. Asked once about where he drew his inspiration from, Poole said, "I'm playing for two."

1993: 7 catches, 119 yards, 1 touchdown
1994: 31 catches, 669 yards, 6 touchdowns
1995: 55 catches, 1,036 yards, 7 touchdowns
1996: 47 catches, 867 yards, 11 touchdowns

MIKE RICHARDSON
Cornerback
1979–1982

Most athletes are fortunate to start two years for a Division I team. Mike Richardson was a four-year starter for the Sun Devils. He was a first-team All-American in 1981 and 1982. He's still ASU's all-time leader in career interceptions with 18. That 1982 team, fueled by his coverage skills and tackling ability—he led the club with 124 stops—allowed more than 20 points only twice in 12 games.

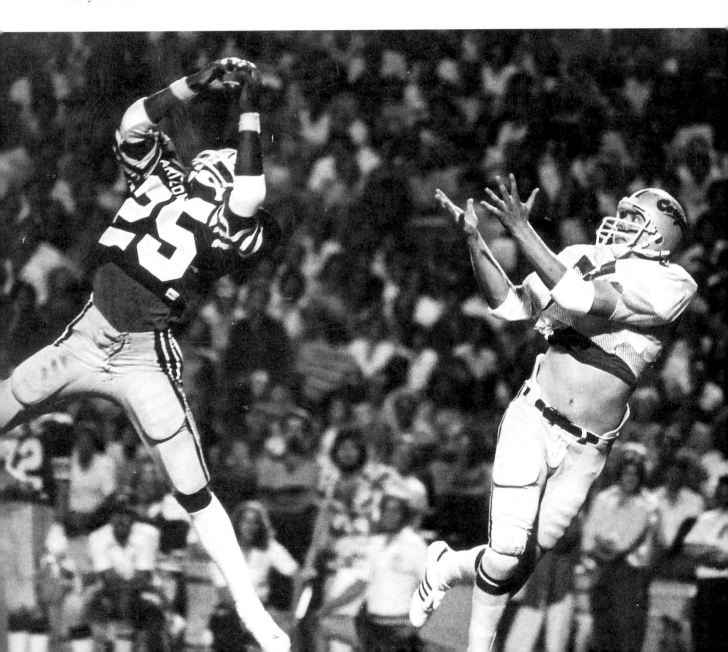

DERRICK RODGERS
Linebacker
1996

No player has made more of an impact in a single season than Rodgers did in 1996. Rodgers didn't even play football in high school—he played trumpet for the band. But what sweet music he was to ASU's ears. A lightly regarded community college recruit, Rodgers led the Pac-10 in tackles for loss (23) and had 12 sacks. He was the most explosive player on a defensive unit that led the Pac-10 in nearly every category and helped the Sun Devils get to the Rose Bowl.

JUAN ROQUE
Tackle
1994–1996

Roque turned down USC to accept a scholarship offer from ASU. The Trojans' loss was ASU's gain. Roque grew into a 6'8", 313-pound bodyguard for Sun Devils' quarterback Jake Plummer. Roque could have left school after his junior season—he already had completed his history degree—but he returned for his senior year. Smart move. ASU went 11–1, played in the Rose Bowl, and Roque was a consensus All-American.

GREY RUEGAMER
Tackle
1995–1998

Grey Ruegamer was best known for the stories he would tell, such as the time he once tasted goat testicles. But Ruegamer could play a little, too. The rare four-year starter on the offensive line, he was an All-Pac-10 center in 1997 and 1998. He was named second-team All-American in 1998 by *Football News* and the Walter Camp Football Foundation. Ruegamer was selected in the third round of the 1999 draft by the Miami Dolphins and has bounced around the NFL, playing for four teams.

Derrick Rodgers

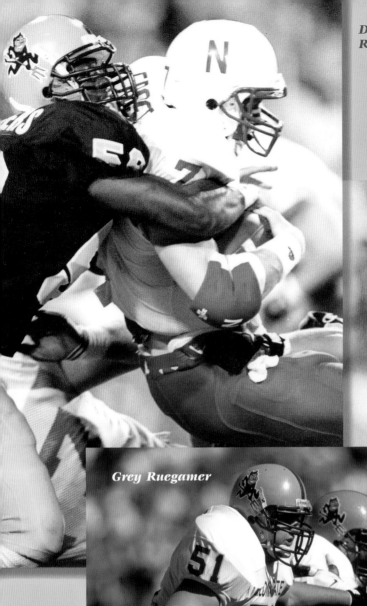

Juan Roque

Grey Ruegamer

Terrell Suggs took home the hardware in 2002, winning the Lombardi, Bronko Nagurski and Ted Hendricks awards.

TERRELL SUGGS
Defensive End
2000–2002

Suggs was a standout two-way player at Chandler Hamilton High School, and some schools wanted him to play fullback. But ASU saw him as a defensive end, and Suggs became the most prolific pass rusher in school history. He had 44 sacks for his career, including an NCAA-record 24 in 2002. That same season Suggs had 31½ tackles for loss, a Sun Devil record. A slow 40-yard dash time diminished Suggs's value in the draft, but the Baltimore Ravens grabbed him with the 10th overall pick, and he was named Defensive Rookie of the Year in 2003. He was named to two Pro Bowls during his first four seasons.

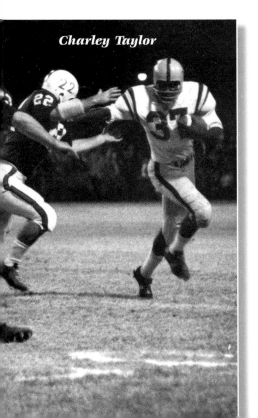

Charley Taylor

CHARLEY TAYLOR
Wide Receiver
1961–1963

Taylor arrived at ASU in the fall of 1960 without a position. The Grand Prairie, Texas, native could play halfback, wide receiver and defensive back. But it took just one look at Taylor leaping over tacklers for coach Frank Kush to move him to wingback.

ASU's teams were so talented that Taylor never led the Sun Devils in rushing or receiving. But his athletic talent was so impressive that the Washington Redskins drafted him in the first round in 1964. Taylor went on to have a brilliant NFL career, playing in four Pro Bowls, leading the NFL in receiving in 1966 and 1967 and retiring as the NFL's all-time leading receiver with 649 catches. In 1984, he became the first Sun Devil to be inducted into the Pro Football Hall of Fame.

1961: 13 catches, 235 yards, 2 touchdowns
1962: 7 catches, 104 yards, 2 touchdowns
1963: 11 catches, 217 yards, 2 touchdowns

DANNY VILLA
Tackle
1984–1986

Villa never said much, but he didn't have to—his ability spoke loud and clear. Villa, a left tackle, was the anchor of an offensive line that helped ASU average 208.7 rushing yards per game in 1986. Villa was named best lineman in the Pac-10 and was a consensus All-American.

DARREN WOODSON
Defensive Back
1989–1991

Darren Woodson doesn't show up on any All-America lists for ASU. He was honorable mention All-Pac-10 three years. But Woodson will always be remembered as a Sun Devil great because of what he accomplished in the NFL. A linebacker at ASU, Woodson was drafted as a safety by the Dallas Cowboys and played in five Pro Bowls. He was a member of Dallas' three championship teams in the 1990s.

LUIS ZENDEJAS
Placekicker
1981–1984

No one could have guessed that the player who broke Tony Dorsett's NCAA scoring record of 356 points would be a pudgy placekicker from Mexico City. But Zendejas wasn't just your average kicker. When he left ASU he held or shared 12 NCAA records. He kicked three or more field goals in a game 13 times. As a junior in 1983, he led the nation with 28 field goals. Zendejas finished his career with 368 points and as the unlikely answer to a trivia question.

Danny Villa

Darren Woodson

Luis Zendejas

Bruce Snyder owned a 58-47 record in nine seasons with ASU.

The Coaches

For the first 58 years of its existence, the Arizona State football program was defined by its mediocrity.

Coaches came and went every few years. Fred Irish, ASU's first coach, was on the sidelines for eight seasons (from 1897 to 1906), and for the next 52 years he would continue to boast the longest tenure of any ASU coach.

Some coaches had more success than others. Dixie Howell led ASU to Border Conference championships in 1939 and 1940, and Clyde Smith won another Border Conference title in 1952.

But in the fall of 1955, two men came to ASU who would lead a renaissance in Sun Devil football. One was the head football coach, the other his assistant.

Together, and over a span of 24 years, they turned ASU into a college football powerhouse.

DAN DEVINE
1955–1957
27–3–1

Devine was only 31 years old when he became Arizona State's head coach in 1955. A Wisconsin native who earned the nickname the "Proctor Flash" for his athletic accomplishments at Proctor High School in Minnesota, Devine had been an assistant coach under Clarence "Biggie" Munn at Michigan State for five years.

ASU's football program was struggling at the time. It had finished 5–5 in 1954 and 4–5–1 in 1953 under Clyde Smith.

Devine, however, turned the program around immediately. He went 8–2–1 in his first year, losing only to San Jose State and archrival Arizona.

Incredibly, that would be Devine's worst year in his three seasons at ASU.

In 1956, the Sun Devils went 9–1, losing only to UTEP, and the following season, they went 10–0, posted four shutouts and led the nation in total offense and scoring. ASU finished the season ranked 12th in the country, the first time in school history the Sun Devils had made the top 25.

The soft-spoken Devine was a self-proclaimed fussbudget who insisted that his players have their shoes shined and their pants pressed, but he also was a progressive thinker. He brought the first black players to ASU.

As for the notion that he wasn't tough like most football coaches of his time, Devine famously said, "Macho, macho, what does that mean? I have six daughters and one son. How much more macho can you be?"

DON DEVINE AT ASU		
YEAR	RECORD	FINAL AP RANK
1955	8–2–1	
1956	9–1	
1957	10–0	12th

FRANK KUSH
1958–1979
176–54–1

There are few coaches in college sports who are synonymous with their universities.

John Wooden and UCLA. Bobby Bowden and Florida State. Mike Krzysewski and Duke.

Frank Kush is ASU.

The field at Sun Devil Stadium bears his name.

The football program is stamped with his signature.

He remains, even today, the most notable figure in ASU athletics history.

Kush wasn't always an icon. When he became the Sun Devils' coach in December of 1957, replacing Dan Devine, he was an anonymous assistant on Devine's staff. There was no way to predict what he would do or who he would become.

Kush has been exceeding expectations his whole life, though. One of 14 children of a Pennsylvania coal miner, he escaped a life in the dark and dust by becoming a 5'7", 150-pound defensive lineman for Michigan State from 1950 to 1952. He was named an All-American his senior year and helped the Spartans win the national championship. He later was inducted into the Michigan State Hall of Fame.

It was at Michigan State that Kush became the no-nonsense, hard-nosed personality that would shape ASU football for the next two decades.

"I was coached that way in high school and at Michigan State," Kush said. "The biggest thing I learned along the way was the importance of fundamentals and the progress players could make if they had good coaches."

Kush couldn't have been more unlike his predecessor at ASU. Devine was a soft-spoken man who always had a smile on his face. Kush was loud, profane and demanding. He wanted his teams to be tougher and more physical than their opponents, and that attitude began with him.

"He was as tough as Charles Finley and George Steinbrenner rolled into one," said baseball Hall of Famer Reggie Jackson, who

FRANK KUSH AT ASU		
YEAR	RECORD	FINAL AP RANK
1958	7–3	
1959	10–1	
1960	7–3	
1961	7–3	
1962	7–2–1	
1963	8–1	
1964	8–2	
1965	6–4	
1966	5–5	
1967	8–2	
1968	8–2	23rd
1969	8–2	
1970	11–0	6th
1971	11–1	8th
1972	10–2	13th
1973	11–1	9th
1974	7–5	
1975	12–0	2nd
1976	4–7	
1977	9–3	18th
1978	9–3	
1979	3–2*	

*Fired midway through season

Frank Kush received a memorable send-off, getting a victory ride from his players following his last game as ASU coach, a 12–7 win over Washington.

went to ASU on a football scholarship in 1965, citing two notoriously strong-willed owners for whom he played.

Kush's legacy needs no embellishment.

He went 176–54–1 during his 22 seasons at ASU. Nineteen of his 22 teams had winning records, and 18 of those won seven games or more. He led the Sun Devils to their first top-10 ranking in school history—No. 6 in 1970—and sent 128 players to the NFL.

In short, he put ASU on the college football map.

Kush also was 6–1 in bowl games and, most importantly, he beat archrival Arizona 16 of 21 times.

Kush was a success right from the start. The 1958 Sun Devils went 7–3, beginning a stretch of seven straight seasons in which his teams won at least seven games.

By 1969, Kush was so well-regarded in college football circles that the University of Pittsburgh offered him its head coaching job. Kush, enticed by the opportunity to return home, accepted the job. Five days later, though, he changed his mind and decided to stay at ASU.

"I like it here," he said simply. "This is where I want to stay."

Kush's change of heart led to the greatest four-year stretch in Sun Devil football history. ASU went 11–0 in 1970, 11–1 in 1971, 10–2 in 1972 and 11–1 in 1973. Cumulative record for those four seasons: 43–4.

It was in 1970 that college football cognoscenti east of the Mississippi discovered ASU. The Western Athletic Conference was lightly regarded at the time, but Kush and the Sun Devils silenced the skeptics with their 48–26 victory over North Carolina in the Peach Bowl.

The next three seasons, ASU would beat Florida State, Missouri and Pittsburgh in the Fiesta Bowl.

By that time, Kush's reputation as an intense, demanding coach was well-known. One of his most infamous coaching techniques was the hamburger drill, in which a player was encircled by teammates and had to

"My job is to win football games. I've got to put people in the stadium, make money for the university, keep the alumni happy, and give the school a winning reputation. If I don't win, I'm gone."

—FRANK KUSH, COACH, 1958–1979

block each one of them one at a time until he collapsed.

A player who did something wrong at Camp Tontozona, site of the Devils' fall training camp, would be forced to run up the nearby mountain. Soon, it became known as Mount Kush.

Doug Decker, a defensive lineman in 1974, said Kush "would pick up a plastic cover in practice and keep hitting players on the rear end with it as they were down in their stance."

While the practice seems cruel now, it was a different time in the 1970s, and most of Kush's players understood that their coach simply was trying to mold them into the best football players they could be.

"Frank Kush was able to get out of me something that no one else could get," said Danny White, ASU's quarterback from 1971 to 1973. "He affected hundreds of athletes that he coached in that same way."

Kush, asked about his tactics, said, "I have slapped kids on the headgear with my hand, and believe me, it hurts my hand a heck of a lot more than it will ever hurt the kids. I want them to look me in the eye."

There's little argument as to what was Kush's greatest single season as ASU's coach, and the greatest season in Arizona State history. In 1975, Kush guided the Sun Devils to a 12–0 record and a 17–14 victory over Nebraska in the

Fiesta Bowl, a game in which his son, Danny, kicked the game-winning field goal.

ASU ended the year ranked No. 2 nationally, angering Sun Devil fans who thought they should have been No. 1 instead of 11–1 Oklahoma.

It seemed, at that point, that Kush could coach as long as he wanted at ASU. He had no desire to go to the NFL—"I felt very comfortable coaching college football," he said—and no one dared question him, much less criticize him, in Arizona.

By 1978, ASU's success under Kush prompted the school's move from the WAC to the Pac-10. But it was also during that season that the beginning of the end came for ASU's coach.

Punter Kevin Rutledge accused Kush of punching him in the face during an October 28 game against Washington. Kush denied the charges.

The alleged incident created a firestorm at ASU. The Rutledge family's attorney received death threats. The insurance office of Rutledge's father suffered a fire.

Kush survived the season, but reporters who once genuflected in his presence began to take a closer look at the ASU program. Soon, reports surfaced that Kush had asked coaches and players to keep quiet about the incident. Some players said they were asked to sign affidavits saying they never saw Kush hit Rutledge.

Kush coached the first four games of the 1979 season as the controversy engulfed the program. But three hours before the October 13 game against Washington, he held a hastily called press conference to announce that he had been fired.

Athletic Director Fred Miller, in explaining the firing, said, "I learned that Frank Kush was attempting to cover up the fact that he hit Kevin Rutledge. I could not allow our athletes and coaches to be further intimidated."

The Sun Devils beat the Huskies, 12–7, and the players carried Kush off the field on their shoulders.

Kush once was asked if, in retrospect, he'd change his tough-guy approach.

"I put on a clinic every year in Alaska," he said, "and I do the same things I've always done. If a kid gets me mad, I get all over his butt."

Kush was inducted into the College Football Hall of Fame in 1995. The following year, at halftime of ASU's 19–0 victory over Nebraska, the field at Sun Devil Stadium was renamed Frank Kush Field.

FRANK KUSH TIMELINE

1955—Kush joins Dan Devine's staff at ASU as assistant coach.

1958—Kush becomes ASU's head coach at the age of 28.

1959—Kush leads ASU to Border Conference championship and 10–1 record.

1968—ASU finishes 8–2 and ranked 23rd in country, first national ranking since 1957.

1970—Sun Devils go 10–0 in regular season, receive first-ever bowl invitation and beat North Carolina, 48–26, in Peach Bowl to finish 11–0 and ranked 6th in country.

1971—ASU plays in first-ever Fiesta Bowl under Kush and beats Florida State, 45–38.

1975—Sun Devils cap off their second 12–0 season by upsetting perennial powerhouse Nebraska, 17–14, in Fiesta Bowl. Kush's son, Danny, kicks game-winning field goal, and ASU finishes year ranked 2nd nationally.

1979—Kush is fired by athletic director Fred Miller three hours before game against Washington. Miller says Kush pressured players and coaches to keep quiet about his allegedly punching punter Kevin Rutledge in the face during 1978 game.

1996—ASU names field at Sun Devil Stadium "Frank Kush Field" during halftime of ASU's 19–0 upset of Nebraska.

John Cooper's brief tenure at Arizona State included the only Rose Bowl win in ASU history.

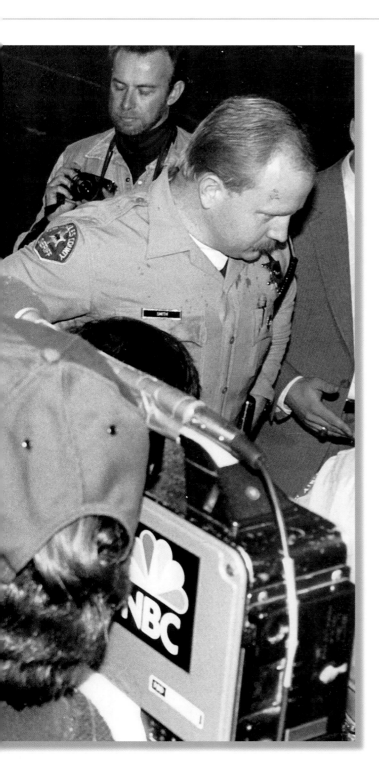

JOHN COOPER
1985–1987
25–9–2

Cooper wasn't at ASU for a long time, but he certainly left an impression.

In just his second season as the Sun Devils' coach, he led ASU to its first-ever Pac-10 title and trip to the Rose Bowl.

The Devils were big underdogs to Big Ten powerhouse Michigan, but ASU overcame an 8–0 first-quarter deficit and won 22–15. The lead in the next day's newspaper read, "Mission Accomplished."

Cooper won his third straight bowl game as ASU's coach the following year, beating Air Force, 33–28, in the Freedom Bowl, and his accomplishments caught the eye of Ohio State, which lured him away from Tempe.

JOHN COOPER AT ASU		
YEAR	RECORD	FINAL AP RANK
1985	8-4	
1986	10-1-1	4th
1987	7-4-1	20th

BRUCE SNYDER
1992–2000
58–47–0

It's unusual for a school to steal a coach from a conference rival, but that's what ASU did in 1992 when it hired Snyder away from California, where he had been Pac-10 Coach of the Year in 1990.

Snyder struggled his first four years at ASU. He failed to lead the Sun Devils to a bowl game and lost three of four games to Arizona. After a 6–5 season in 1995, there were calls for Snyder's firing.

But the boos turned to cheers in 1996 when Snyder and ASU shocked the college football world. First came a 19–0 upset of No. 1 Nebraska on September 21. That was just the preamble, though.

The Sun Devils, led by quarterback Jake Plummer and a tenacious defense featuring Pat Tillman, won their second Pac-10 title and another trip to the Rose Bowl. ASU was within 100 seconds of a national championship when Plummer scored with 1:40 left, but Ohio State marched downfield and won on a David Boston touchdown reception.

Snyder followed up the Rose Bowl trip with a bid to the Sun Bowl in 1997, but he went just 16–18 the following three years and was fired after the 2000 campaign.

BILL KAJIKAWA

Bill Kajikawa never coached a game for the Arizona State varsity. But no coach has had a more lasting impact on Sun Devil athletics than the man everybody calls "Kaji."

Kajikawa received his master's degree in 1937, the same year he became coach of the ASU freshman football team. The Sun Devils were known as the Bulldogs then.

He took a hiatus from ASU to serve in the Army's 442nd Regimental Combat Team, then returned to the university, where he earned a master's degree in 1948.

Kajikawa served under nine ASU head football coaches. He also was the head basketball coach from 1948 to 1957, and the head baseball coach from 1947 to 1957. Not surprisingly, the gentle Kajikawa was inducted into the ASU Hall of Distinction in 1982.

Kajikawa, who retired in 1978, has his fingerprints all over the Sun Devil athletic program. The Sun Devil football team practices on the Kajikawa Practice Field, and his daughter, Christine Wilkinson, is a long-time administrator in ASU's athletic department. She was the Sun Devils' interim AD in 1995–1996 and again in 2000.

Bruce Snyder

BRUCE SNYDER AT ASU

YEAR	RECORD	FINAL AP RANK
1992	6–5	
1993	6–5	
1994	3–8	
1995	6–5	
1996	11–1	4th
1997	9–3	14th
1998	5–6	
1999	6–6	
2000	6–6	

Bill Kajikawa

Jeff Van Raaphorst in the 1987 Rose Bowl.

Sun Devil Superlatives

Through the 2006 season, Arizona State has won 530 varsity football games and 15 conference titles, coming oh-so-close to a national championship in 1996.

One of ASU's biggest football achievements, for which it is rarely given credit, was being instrumental in the Fiesta Bowl's meteoric rise from fledgling postseason game to Bowl Championship Series contest. The Fiesta was, for the most part, created for ASU, and the Sun Devils played in five of the first eight games at Sun Devil Stadium—including the dramatic 1975 contest against Nebraska that put ASU and the bowl itself on the map.

THE GREATEST GAMES

We'll get to the 1975 Fiesta Bowl, which many consider the school's landmark win, in a moment. But when discussing the Sun Devils' best-ever contests, one must start with the game—and more specifically, the play—that ASU faithful remember more often and more fondly than any other in the school's history:

November 29, 1975
ASU 24, Arizona 21
"The Catch"

Those are words that, when spoken anywhere else in the country, invoke the image of Dwight Clark leaping high to pull in Joe Montana's pass for the winning score in the 1981 NFC Championship game.

ASU fans, however, know that John Jefferson inspired the name first. His acrobatic touchdown reception is the most memorable—and controversial—play of what is considered the greatest game between the Sun Devils and archrival Arizona.

That score propelled ASU to a victory that clinched an unbeaten regular season, a Western Athletic Conference championship and a Fiesta Bowl berth.

Jefferson's touchdown, which came in the final minute of the first half, cut a 14–3 Arizona lead to only four points and shifted momentum to the Sun Devils in a game in which the stakes were sky-high.

ASU was 10–0 and ranked eighth in the nation. The Wildcats—who a year earlier broke the Sun Devils' nine-game winning streak in the series—came to Tempe with a 9–1 record and No. 11 national ranking.

"It's probably the game our fans remember most vividly because it was a close ballgame between two great college football teams," Arizona State head coach Frank Kush said. "The rivalry was there full-force, which is how it should be."

Quarterback Dennis Sproul led a Sun Devil march to the Arizona 8-yard line with 30 seconds remaining in the second quarter. Having lined up to the left in the formation, Jefferson quickly cut inside on a slant route as Sproul released the ball.

"John laid his body out, three or four feet off the ground, and caught it," Kush said. "I can still see the official putting his hands in the air to signal a touchdown."

Without question, the diving Jefferson plucked the ball out of the air. But it popped out when his elbows hit the ground—the major pillar of a catch-denying case that is still argued in Tucson.

"I know I did catch the ball," said Jefferson, who had another touchdown catch in the second half. "No doubt, the ball was caught. The referee said it was a touchdown, and that was the end of it."

"The Catch" secured Jefferson's place in the pantheon of ASU gridiron gods.

"Beating Nebraska probably gave us more national recognition than any game we had played prior to that," Kush said. "But without that win (over Arizona), it wouldn't have been possible."

Hey, if the Godfather of ASU football believes it to be the most important game in school history, we certainly won't argue.

Is this the greatest catch in college football history? You be the judge.

The kick that put Sun Devil football on the national map: Danny Kush's game-winner in the 1975 Fiesta Bowl win over Nebraska.

Fiesta Bowl
'Tune in America'

Arizona State vs. Nebraska
December 26, 1975

1975 Fiesta Bowl Dec. 26

'76

Fifth Edition
Fiesta Bowl Magazine
$1.50

1975 Fiesta Bowl
ASU 17, Nebraska 14

But the Sun Devil dramatics were not over in 1975, as ASU outlasted national power Nebraska to finish the season ranked second in the nation. The hero in this game was a player who remains near and dear to coach Frank Kush, but before he could take center stage, the Sun Devils had to overcome a 14–6 fourth-quarter deficit.

ASU did just that on a touchdown pass from Fred Mortensen to John Jefferson and subsequent two-point conversion. That set up the heroics of Danny Kush, the coach's son, who late in the fourth quarter broke the tie with a 29-yard field goal. A defensive stand later, the Sun Devils were Fiesta Bowl champions.

"Not only was this game important for the recognition this team will receive," Kush said, "but it also helps gain recognition for the great teams and players we have had here in the past."

October 14, 1978
ASU 20, Southern California 7

The Sun Devils were fresh out of the WAC, playing their first season among the bigger boys in the Pac-10. And on a Saturday night at Sun Devil Stadium, the biggest of the boys paid a visit.

Actually, these boys were men. As in the men of Troy. Among them were Charles White, a future Heisman Trophy winner, and Anthony Munoz and Ronnie Lott, future NFL Hall of Famers. Twenty USC starters went on to NFL careers. How could the Sun Devils possibly expect to stay with these guys?

Not only did they stay with the Trojans, they dominated them, handing a USC team that would eventually win a share of the national title its only defeat of the season. Quarterback Mark Malone ran and passed for a touchdown, and USC's only score came on a touchdown pass with 33 seconds remaining.

Jubilant ASU fans celebrated the triumph by dancing in the streets of downtown Tempe, but Kush—evidently unimpressed and furious over the lost shutout—put his team through a miserable series of practices the following week.

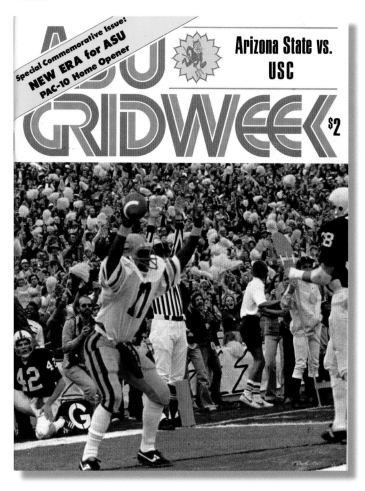

1987 Rose Bowl
ASU 22, Michigan 15

After blowing two previous chances to play in "The Granddaddy of Them All"—ASU losses against Arizona in 1982 and 1985 denied the Sun Devils Pac-10 titles—the third time was a charm in 1986.

But when a national television audience first tuned into college football's most prestigious game, the Wolverines appeared to be on their way to their second Rose Bowl win in eight visits under Coach Bo Schembechler.

Michigan controlled the early portion of the game, putting together two long touchdown drives in the game's first 20 minutes. At the same time, John Cooper's Sun Devils managed only two field goal attempts, one of which was converted.

After the Wolverines pushed their advantage to 15–3, the game's complexion changed. The Sun Devils roared back with 10 points before halftime. ASU's first touchdown closed the gap to 15–13 with 29 seconds left in the second quarter, coming on a 1-yard touchdown pass from Jeff Van Raaphorst to Bruce Hill.

The second half was all ASU. Hill tiptoed along the back of the end zone with his second touchdown reception, giving the Sun Devils their first lead in the third quarter. Kent Bostrom added a record-tying third field goal in the fourth quarter. The Sun Devil defense consistently smothered Michigan's offense, ending its last drive with an interception. Van Raaphorst, ASU's senior quarterback, was named the game's most valuable player.

"This is the biggest dang victory I've ever been associated with," Cooper said. "I don't want to sit down. I'm on cloud nine!"

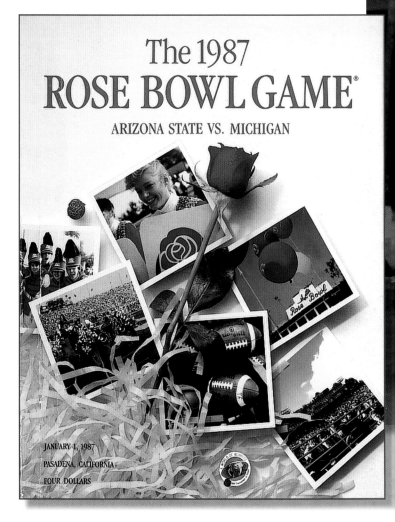

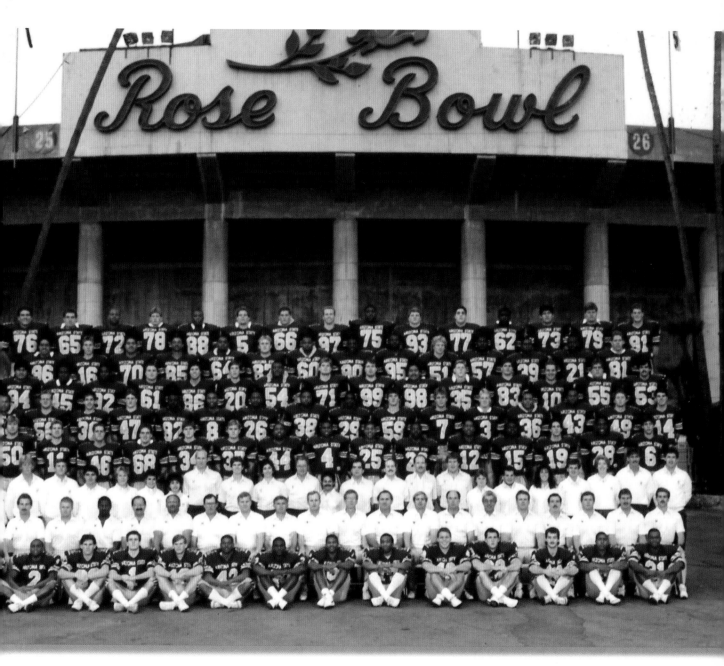

Sun Devils 1987 Rose Bowl team

The Devils shocked the world with their 19–0 shutout of defending national champion Nebraska.

September 21, 1996
ASU 19, Nebraska 0

Just like in that 1978 game against USC, there supposedly was no way the Sun Devils could hang with this opponent.

Nebraska was a 23-point favorite. It was not only unbeaten and ranked No. 1, but it had also won 26 straight games—37 straight in the regular season.

The previous year, the Cornhuskers embarrassed their competition en route to a national title. Those 1995 Cornhuskers—who finished their season in Sun Devil Stadium with a rout of Florida in the Fiesta Bowl—are still regarded as one of history's greatest teams.

In fact, the seeds of ASU's upset were sown during that season. The Cornhuskers had blasted the Sun Devils, 77–28, in Lincoln, Nebraska.

At a team meeting the night before the 1996 game, the players asked the coaches to leave. Various leaders including quarterback Jake Plummer, linebacker Pat Tillman and receiver Keith Poole spoke.

Then Derek Smith, an intense though quiet linebacker, got up.

"I got something to say," Smith said.

Smith, according to numerous accounts, gave such an impassioned, us-against-the-world, nobody-gives-us-a-chance pep talk that his face turned red.

"By the end of it, I had chill bumps," receiver Courtney Jackson said.

After Smith's talk, various accounts have tables being knocked over, at least one chair flying at the chalkboard and players singing the fight song.

In a pregame ceremony, ASU named the field at Sun Devil Stadium after Frank Kush, and on the opening drive, ASU took the ball 80 yards in 10 plays, capped by Plummer finding Poole wide open for a 25-yard score. It was the game's only touchdown.

After the Huskers got the ball, they were pushed back to their own 7-yard line on a holding penalty. Running back Ahman Green couldn't handle a pitchout in the end zone; the ball bounced out of bounds for a safety. By halftime, the Devils led by a stunning 17-0 margin.

Nebraska never erased the goose egg from the scoreboard, and as the clock wound down, ASU center Kirk Robertson, now a pediatric dentist in Flagstaff, Arizona recalled one of Nebraska's players walking up to him and saying, "You guys are legit."

The Sun Devils affirmed their legitimacy with an unbeaten regular season and Pac-10 title, and entered the Rose Bowl with a shot at finishing No. 1.

1997 Rose Bowl
Ohio State 20, ASU 17

With the clock ticking down and a national championship hanging in the balance, Plummer put the finishing touches on his amazing Sun Devil career. Flushed out of the pocket, he took off downfield and—with the help of a deft juke of All-America Ohio State linebacker Andy Katzenmoyer—dove into the end zone for a scintillating 11-yard touchdown run.

ASU 17, Ohio State 14. One minute, 40 seconds remaining. Finally, a program with much success but still a secret to most of the nation would have its coronation on one of football's grandest stages.

Not quite.

"Everyone was real excited except for me," Plummer said. "I was worried the whole time."

Enter Joe Germaine, the Buckeyes' quarterback and native of Mesa, Arizona, who led his team on a 12-play, 65-yard drive that culminated with David Boston's catch in the end zone with 19 seconds remaining.

Destiny denied.

Jake Plummer and the Sun Devils fell 19 seconds short of a national championship.

Sun Devils 1997 Rose Bowl team

The 83rd

Rose Bowl Game

January 1, 1997, Pasadena, California

ARIZONA STATE
vs
OHIO STATE

ROSE BOWL 97

1997 OFFICIAL SOUVENIR ROSE BOWL GAME PROGRAM $ 10.00 TAX INCLUDED

Arizona State's Keegan Herring (No. 24) tries to avoid the tackle by Rutgers' Courtney Greene (No. 36) in the first half of the 2005 Insight Bowl (right). Zach Miller celebrates a touchdown in ASU's 45–40 victory over Rutgers (below).

2005 Insight Bowl
ASU 45, Rutgers 40

When your school helps set a record for most combined yardage ever amassed in a bowl game, it goes down as a memorable contest.

On a night that featured 1,213 yards of offense between the two teams, ASU won a second straight postseason contest for the first time since the 1986 and 1987 seasons. The previous record of 1,158 yards was set by Hawaii and Houston in the 2003 Hawaii Bowl.

Redshirt freshman quarterback Rudy Carpenter hung in after frequent hits from an aggressive Scarlet Knights' front seven to complete 23-of-35 passes for 467 yards and four touchdowns. He was chosen the offensive player of the game.

The last touchdown toss, a 42-yard bomb to senior receiver Matt Miller, put the Sun Devils ahead for good. Miller outleaped safety Ron Girault for his second score of the game, and with a two-point conversion, ASU led 39–33. Miller finished with 135 yards on five receptions.

On the Scarlet Knights' next possession, the Sun Devil faithful among the crowd of 43,536 at Chase Field—home of the Arizona Diamondbacks and nine miles from the ASU campus—became a factor. The noise contributed heavily to a pair of Rutgers false starts that resulted in a third-and-18 situation, and a punt ended the series.

ASU took the ball and marched 69 yards in eight plays to lead by 12 after Rudy Burgess's 4-yard touchdown run. Burgess, who had 125 yards rushing in the 2004 Sun Bowl, rushed for 102 yards.

Rutgers scored a touchdown with two minutes remaining, but Sun Devil tight end Zach Miller recovered the ensuing onside kick, and ASU ran out the clock.

ASU outside linebacker Jamar Williams was named defensive player of the game.

"We told the guys from the get-go that Rutgers would be excited, and of course, we were excited too," Sun Devils coach Dirk Koetter said. "Rutgers had a lot to prove because they haven't been in a bowl game for a while, and they are well-coached and played hard.

"But that doesn't diminish the fact that our guys know how to compete, were ready to compete and put in a hard-fought game."

THE GREAT TEAMS

1957: Dan Devine's Peak

In 1955, ASU gave Dan Devine, an assistant at Michigan State University, his first head coaching job. With the help of a fellow Spartans' assistant Devine convinced to come to Tempe with him—Frank Kush—it took only three seasons for his innovative offense to take the West by storm.

The 1957 team finished 10–0 and featured quarterback Bobby Mulgado—one of only six players to have his number retired by the school—at the controls of the nation's leader in scoring and total offense. The Sun Devils averaged 40 points per game and hit their stride in late October, outscoring their last six opponents by a combined 271–27.

After that season, Devine accepted the coaching job at Missouri. Kush was promoted to ASU's head-coaching position, setting the wheels in motion for his transformation into the face of the athletic department—if not the entire university.

1957 (10–0)

Coach Dan Devine
Arizona State 28, Wichita State 0
Arizona State 19, Idaho 7
Arizona State 44, San Jose State 6
Arizona State 35, Hardin-Simmons 26
Arizona State 66, San Diego State 0
Arizona State 21, New Mexico State 0
Arizona State 43, Texas-El Paso 7
Arizona State 53, Montana State 13
Arizona State 41, Pacific 0
Arizona State 47, Arizona 7

A rare sight: the Sun Devils in the snow, in the 1970 Peach Bowl win over North Carolina.

1969–1972: Four straight WAC titles

The Kush era hit its peak of consistency in the late 1960s, with four straight conference titles.

The year before the string started, 1968, ASU had no bowl bid to show for an 8-2 record, thanks to Arizona coach Darrell Mudra's infamous threat to the Sun Bowl to "take us now or lose us" before the rivalry game against ASU in Tucson. (The Sun first intended to select the ASU-UA winner).

The Sun Bowl extended an invitation to the Wildcats, and ASU responded by thumping Arizona 30-7 in what came to be known as the "Ultimatum Bowl." A bowl-less Sun Devil team was the last straw for some Phoenix-area sports bigwigs, who began formulating plans for the creation of the Fiesta Bowl three years later.

In 1970, the Sun Devils went 11–0 and defeated North Carolina in the Peach Bowl, a game that was played in snow.

1969 (8–2)

Coach Frank Kush

Arizona State 48, Minnesota 26
Oregon State 30, Arizona State 7
Arizona State 23, Brigham Young 7
Utah 24, Arizona State 23
Arizona State 45, San Jose State 11
Arizona State 30, Wyoming 14
Arizona State 48, New Mexico 17
Arizona State 42, Texas-El Paso 19
Arizona State 79, Colorado State 7
Arizona State 38, Arizona 24

ASU—with such notable players as quarterback Danny White, running backs Woody Green and Ben Malone, defensive end Junior Ah You and cornerback Mike Haynes—appeared in the first three Fiesta Bowls (1971–1973), all victories.

1970 Sun Devils

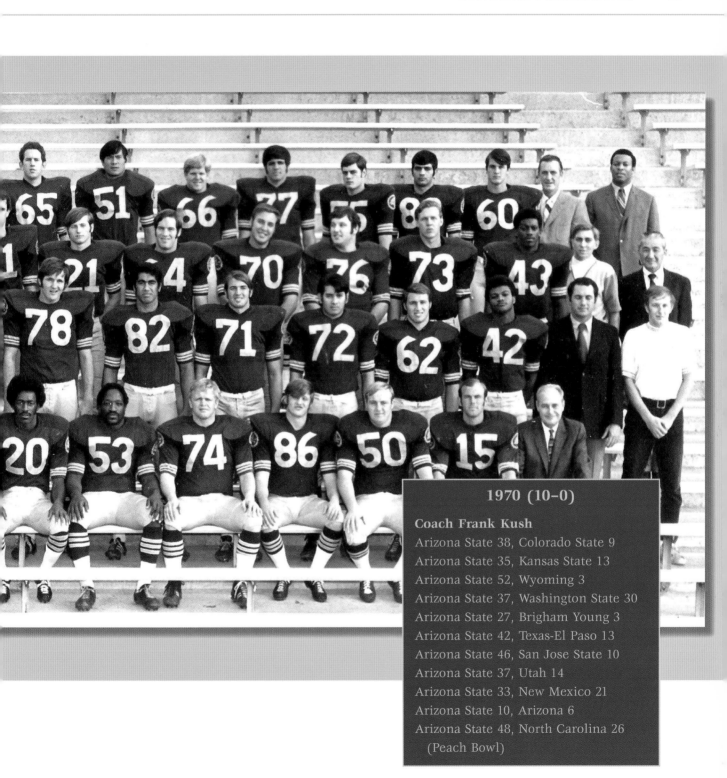

1970 (10–0)

Coach Frank Kush
Arizona State 38, Colorado State 9
Arizona State 35, Kansas State 13
Arizona State 52, Wyoming 3
Arizona State 37, Washington State 30
Arizona State 27, Brigham Young 3
Arizona State 42, Texas-El Paso 13
Arizona State 46, San Jose State 10
Arizona State 37, Utah 14
Arizona State 33, New Mexico 21
Arizona State 10, Arizona 6
Arizona State 48, North Carolina 26
  (Peach Bowl)

1971 (11–1)

Coach Frank Kush
Arizona State 18, Houston 17
Arizona State 41, Utah 21
Arizona State 24, Texas-El Paso 7
Arizona State 42, Colorado State 0
Oregon State 24, Arizona State 18
Arizona State 60, New Mexico 28
Arizona State 44, Air Force 28
Arizona State 38, Brigham Young 13
Arizona State 52, Wyoming 19
Arizona State 49, San Jose State 6
Arizona State 31, Arizona 0
Arizona State 45, Florida State 38
 (Fiesta Bowl)

1971 Sun Devils

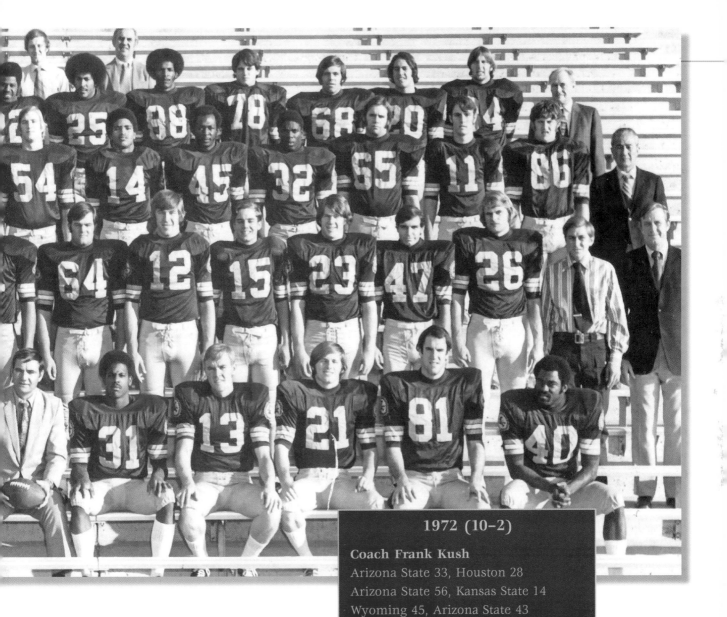

1972 (10–2)

Coach Frank Kush
Arizona State 33, Houston 28
Arizona State 56, Kansas State 14
Wyoming 45, Arizona State 43
Arizona State 38, Oregon State 7
Arizona State 59, Utah 48
Arizona State 49, Brigham Young 17
Air Force 39, Arizona State 31
Arizona State 55, Texas-El Paso 14
Arizona State 60, New Mexico 7
Arizona State 51, San Jose State 21
Arizona State 38, Arizona 21
Arizona State 49, Missouri 35
 (Fiesta Bowl)

1975: America, meet ASU

Despite its incredible success in the WAC, ASU remained a secret to the rest of the nation. That all changed in 1975, when the Sun Devils raced to wins in their first 10 games, then earned a dramatic victory against Arizona, thanks to John Jefferson's heroics.

With another conference title in hand, ASU readied for a Fiesta Bowl date against Big Eight co-champion Nebraska, to be nationally televised on CBS. The 17-14 Sun Devil victory meant that their legitimacy was beamed to the entire nation. ASU finished No. 2 in both wire service polls, and *The Sporting News* selected the Sun Devils as its national champion.

Among the future NFL players on the 1975 team were Jefferson, cornerback Mike Haynes, tight end Bruce Hardy, receiver Larry Mucker, linebacker Larry Gordon and safety John Harris.

1975 (12–0)

Coach Frank Kush

Arizona State 35, Washington 12
Arizona State 33, Texas Christian 10
Arizona State 20, Brigham Young 0
Arizona State 29, Idaho 3
Arizona State 16, New Mexico 10
Arizona State 33, Colorado State 3
Arizona State 24, Texas-El Paso 6
Arizona State 40, Utah 14
Arizona State 21, Wyoming 20
Arizona State 55, Pacific 14
Arizona State 24, Arizona 21
Arizona State 17, Nebraska 14
  (Fiesta Bowl)

1986: Finally, ASU grabs the Roses

Darryl Rogers, after leaving Tempe to become head coach of the NFL's Detroit Lions, bequeathed to his successor a roster loaded with talented recruits. That successor was John Cooper, and ASU's talent, maximized by the motivation of Cooper and his assistants, resulted in the school's first Pac-10 championship.

The 1986 Sun Devils were obscenely talented, with offensive linemen Randall McDaniel and Danny Villa, wide receiver Aaron Cox, defensive linemen Trace Armstrong and Dan Saleaumua and cornerback Eric Allen among the 17 future NFL players on the roster.

"Look at the number of guys from the 1986 team who went to the NFL and compare them to other years at ASU," said quarterback Jeff Van Raaphorst. "Trace Armstrong had a nice career in the NFL, but he had to fight for playing time on our team."

The 1986 season began with a 20–17 victory against Michigan State, and ASU hit its stride winning three straight road games—including at UCLA and USC. The Sun Devils became the first Pac-10 team to beat both schools in Los Angeles/Pasadena in the same season. A 49–0 rout against California clinched the Rose Bowl bid, meaning the result of the season-ending game against Arizona didn't matter in the conference standings.

ASU lost to Arizona, but completed the season in grand fashion with a 22–15 victory against Big Ten champion Michigan on January 1. The Sun Devils were ranked fourth in the final polls.

Cooper would play a vital role in ASU football history a decade later in the same stadium—standing on the other sideline.

Eric Allen was an integral part of the 1986 Sun Devils.

1986 (10–1–1)

Coach John Cooper
Arizona State 20, Michigan State 17
Arizona State 30, SMU 0
Arizona State 21, Washington State 21
Arizona State 16, UCLA 9
Arizona State 37, Oregon 17
Arizona State 29, Southern California 20
Arizona State 52, Utah 7
Arizona State 34, Washington 21
Arizona State 49, California 0
Arizona State 52, Wichita State 6
Arizona 34, Arizona State 17
Arizona State 22, Michigan 15
  (Rose Bowl)

1996: 19 seconds short

In terms of excitement, drama and human emotion, this might be the best ASU football season of all. The team's heart (quarterback Jake Plummer, who finished third in the Heisman Trophy balloting) and soul (linebacker Pat Tillman, the Pac-10's Defensive Player of the Year who was later killed in combat in Afghanistan) guided the Sun Devils to the precipice of a national championship.

Only Ohio State's touchdown with 19 seconds remaining for a 20–17 victory in the Rose Bowl denied ASU a No. 1 finish. That Buckeyes team was coached by John Cooper.

"There is no magic or destiny in football," said Juan Roque, an offensive lineman on the 1996 team. "It starts with the players being on the same page as the coaching staff. What separated 1996 from my other years at ASU was the fact that everyone was on board."

There was a lot of adversity to overcome. The Sun Devils had three grueling games against league opponents, beating Washington on a last-second field goal, coming back to win at UCLA and outlasting Southern California in double overtime.

Plummer, nicknamed "The Snake," was at his slithering best in the game at UCLA, throwing for a touchdown, running for another and catching one on a halfback option pass. As in 1986, a home-field rout of California clinched the Rose Bowl berth, but Arizona would not spoil the celebration this time. The Sun Devils drilled the Wildcats 56–14 in Tucson, after which coach Bruce Snyder made it abundantly clear where he felt ASU should be ranked.

"We're No. 1," Snyder said. "I have a vote (in the coaches' poll), and I'm voting us No. 1."

The Rose Bowl proved that ASU had the talent to finish on top. All it lacked was the timing—more precisely, 19 seconds' worth.

1996 (11–1)

Coach Bruce Snyder
Arizona State 45, Washington 42
Arizona State 52, North Texas 7
Arizona State 19, Nebraska 0
Arizona State 48, Oregon 27
Arizona State 56, Boise State 7
Arizona State 42, UCLA 34
Arizona State 48, Southern California 35 (2OT)
Arizona State 41, Stanford 9
Arizona State 29, Oregon State 14
Arizona State 35, California 7
Arizona State 56, Arizona 14
Ohio State 20, Arizona State 17 (Rose Bowl)

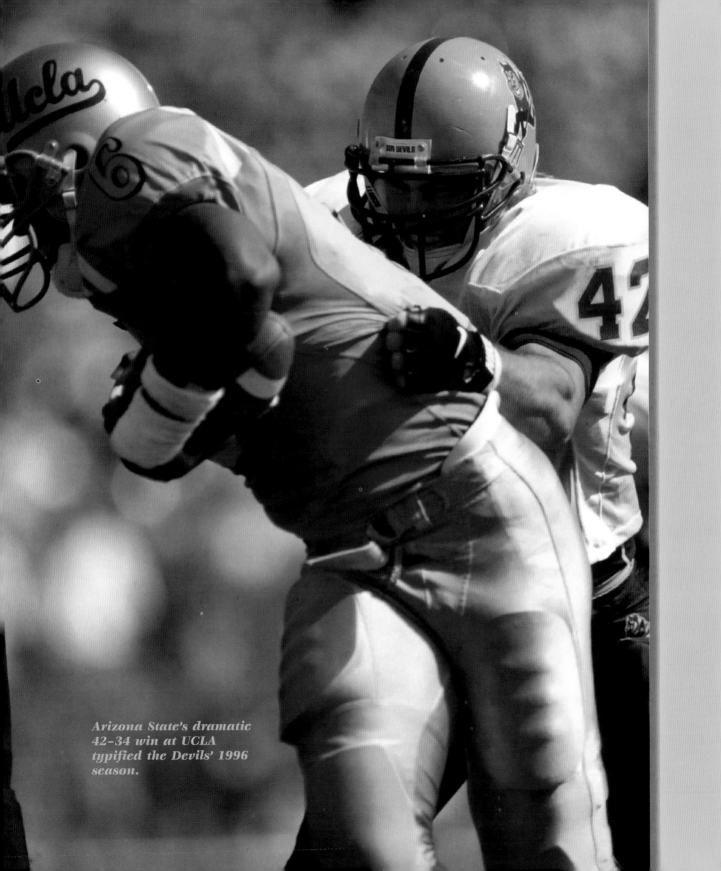

Arizona State's dramatic 42–34 win at UCLA typified the Devils' 1996 season.

The Devils posted a decisive 28–14 win over Arizona in Tucson in 2006.

The Rivalries

I t's a 109-mile drive down Interstate 10 from the campus of Arizona State University to the University of Arizona.

The trip takes less than two hours, traffic permitting. It's a boring drive, with little to look at along the road, unless you consider the truck stop in Toltec a scenic vista.

But so many stories have been told over the years on those 109 miles. Stories of triumph and heartbreak, of hostility and friendship, of unexpected plays and even unlikelier heroes.

Some Arizona State fans, mindful of the fact the University of Arizona has never played in the Rose Bowl, like to pretend that USC has become the Sun Devils' main rival.

But any true ASU fan knows that's not true.

There's only one rivalry game for Arizona State. Only one game that ignites the passions and stirs the soul.

And to think, it all started because ASU was denied university status in the 1950s.

ASU VS. ARIZONA

A 1954 report by Dr. E. V. Hollis, chief of college administration for the U.S. Office of Education, recommended that Arizona State College at Tempe be designated a university.

The report didn't sit well with University of Arizona president Richard Harvill, who said, "For the survey staff to say ASCT is a university does not make it so."

In November of that year, the Arizona Board of Regents met to vote on the recommendation. The regents aligned along old, factional lines, and governor Howard Pyle broke the tie in ASCT's favor.

That same day, the Arizona football team beat ASU, 57–14, but "nobody cared," according to Alfred Thomas and Ernest Hopkins, who wrote *The Arizona State University Story.*

That would be the last time the game meant so little.

The rivalry between the two schools actually began in 1899, when the Territorial Normal School at Tempe beat Arizona, 11–2. Arizona won 20 of the next 21 games, however.

Eventually, the ASU program would close the gap on its rival from the south. The all-time series stands at 35–44–1.

But numbers don't come close to defining the ASU-UA war. One columnist called it the nastiest rivalry in the country. Others have said it is the Southwest's version of Auburn-Alabama or Ohio State-Michigan.

Each year, Arizona fans sneak up "A" mountain just west of Sun Devil Stadium and try to paint the gold "A" red and blue. Arizona State fraternities have taken to guarding the mountain the week before the game in an effort to blunt the Wildcat artists.

There's little doubt about the significance of the game for the two schools, or how much enmity exists between fans, players and even coaches.

Former Arizona coach Dick Tomey referred to the Sun Devils as "those guys." When Larry Smith became UA's head coach in 1980, he

erected a sign outside his office with four yearly goals:

1. Have fun.
2. Get an education.
3. Win the Rose Bowl.
4. Beat ASU.

The Sun Devils felt the same way about the Wildcats.

Legendary ASU coach Frank Kush often said he hated Arizona. Former Sun Devils quarterback Danny White hasn't set foot in Tucson since he ended his college playing career in 1973.

Dirk Koetter, ASU's coach from 2001 to 2006, recalled being stopped in a grocery store in 2005 by an ASU fan who told him he could not continue living if the Wildcats won that year.

"The general dislike among the fans is far greater than I anticipated," Koetter said. "The dislike there is almost out of proportion with what it should be."

The two schools play for the Territorial Cup, which the NCAA has recognized as the nation's oldest victory prize.

Winning the Cup generally means a coach has had a good year, but not always. ASU beat Arizona, 28–14, in November of 2006 to clinch a third consecutive postseason berth, but Koetter was fired the next day.

"Make sure that you (don't say), 'Just beat Arizona, because that's all you have to do to keep everybody happy,' because we know that's not true," Koetter said.

The competition between the two schools truly heated up when Kush became the Sun Devils' coach in 1958. Competitive and feisty

Nothing's more satisfying than winning the Territorial Cup on enemy turf, as the Devils did in 2006.

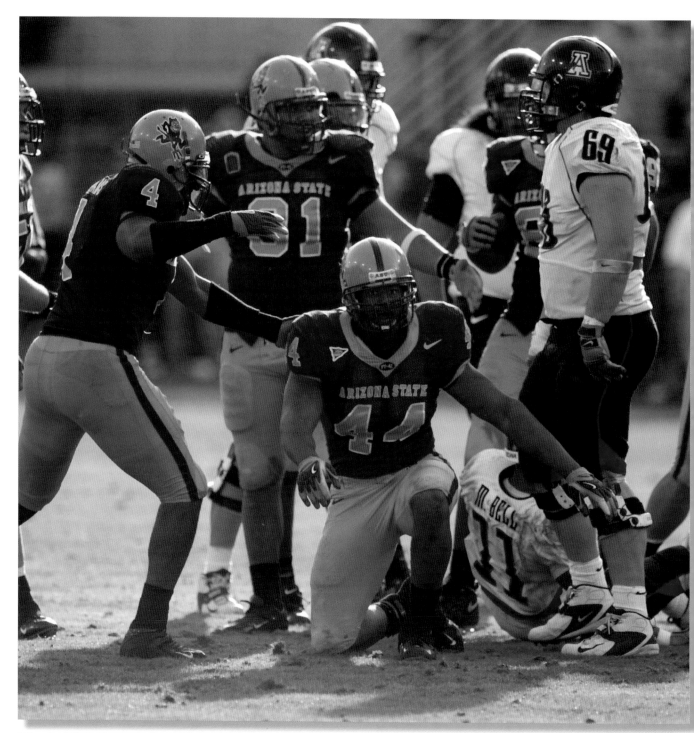

The Devil defense keyed the stunning 23-20 comeback win over Arizona in 2005.

to the core, Kush would rather have cut off a leg than lose to the Wildcats.

"You have to have that feeling, that emotion, and you've got to learn to hate those SOBs," Kush said before the 1996 game between the two schools.

The Sun Devils fed off Kush's hostility and dominated the Wildcats during his 21 years as coach. Kush went 16–5 against Arizona, including a streak of nine straight wins from 1965 to 1973.

Ironically, it was one of those wins that forever changed the bowl landscape.

In 1968 Sun Bowl officials offered to extend an invitation to the ASU–UA winner. Arizona officials balked, saying they wanted an offer before the game. The Sun Bowl gave in, and UA got the bid even though it lost to ASU, 30–7.

At the Sun Devils' team banquet following the season, university president G. Homer Durham, frustrated by the turn of events, made an offhand remark that ASU needed its own bowl game. Three years later, the first Fiesta Bowl was played.

Arizona fans have done their share of grumbling over the years, but never more so than in 1975. ASU was 10–0 and ranked No. 8 heading into the game; UA 9–1 and ranked No. 11.

The Sun Devils won the game, 24–21, but that's not what sticks in the craw of the Wildcats to this day.

With 30 seconds left in the first half, ASU wide receiver John Jefferson stretched out in midair to attempt to catch a Dennis Sproul pass in the end zone. Jefferson caught the ball and landed on the turf.

The play was called a touchdown and immortalized in ASU lore as "The Catch." But UA players and coaches have always believed Jefferson lost possession when he hit the ground.

"I don't think it was a valid touchdown," Wildcats safety Dennis Anderson said. "He had to dive for the ball that was thrown three feet away from him, and I don't think he ever had it. From where I was, the ball slipped through him."

Arizona would get its revenge—and then some. The Wildcats won eight of nine games—the other was a 24–24 tie in 1987—from 1982 to 1990.

Even the tie didn't pacify Sun Devil fans. ASU had a 24–21 lead with seconds left. All it needed to do was punt the ball and defend a Hail Mary pass to snap a five-game losing streak to the Wildcats.

But there was miscommunication on the play. Long snapper Eddie Grant didn't hear coaches instruct the players to take a delay-of-game penalty. Instead, he snapped the ball to punter Mike Schuh, who fumbled the snap he wasn't expecting and then, to make matters worse, tried to kick it when it was on the ground, resulting in a 15-yard penalty.

That led to a game-tying 30-yard field goal by UA placekicker Gary Coston.

"I probably think of that play the way Americans think of Pearl Harbor," Schuh said. "It's something that happened that I wish hadn't happened. But it will always be there."

Those were the dark days for ASU—Kush had been fired in 1979—but two of the contests were particularly hard to digest.

The 1982 Sun Devils were 10–1 when they traveled to Tucson on November 27. All they needed to secure a berth in the Rose Bowl was a win over a 5–4–1 Arizona team. But Wildcats quarterback Tom Tunicliffe threw 92- and 65-yard touchdown passes and UA cruised to a 28–18 win.

Three years later, to the absolute disgust of ASU fans, the Wildcats did it again. The Sun Devils, under coach John Cooper, had only one Pac-10 loss heading into their November 23 encounter with Arizona. The game was played in Tempe, but the heartbreak was all too familiar.

Arizona's special teams scored all 16 points in its 16–13 victory over ASU. The Wildcats recovered a fumbled punt for a touchdown, and Max Zendejas kicked three field goals, including a 57-yarder.

"Everybody tells me there are only two things that matter in ASU football—beating the UA and going to the Rose Bowl," Cooper said.

That year, ASU did neither.

There are certain names that don't play well in Tempe. Chuck Cecil is one of them.

In 1986, Cecil picked off a Jeff Van Raaphorst pass six yards deep in his end zone and went 106 yards for a touchdown to spark Arizona to a 34–17 victory.

The Sun Devils still made it to the Rose Bowl that season, where they beat Michigan, 22–15, but Cecil's interception return pains Van Raaphorst to this day.

Like any college football rivalry, the Sun Devils and Wildcats have played some memorable games. They've also had a few duds, particularly in the early part of this decade, when both programs have struggled to stay above .500.

The series also has created some unlikely heroes.

Kevin Galbreath is not a name that will go down in ASU history, but in 1992, against Arizona's famed "Desert Swarm" defense, he became a star.

Normally a special teams player, Galbreath found himself in the lineup because of a series of injuries to ASU's running backs.

The Sun Devils trailed 6–0 in the fourth quarter when Galbreath took a handoff, broke a tackle at the line of scrimmage and went 51 yards for a touchdown and the 7–6 victory.

That game also produced one of the stranger statistics in the history of the ASU program. The Sun Devils ran a grand total of three plays inside Arizona territory—and won.

For the most part, save for an occasional incident between boorish or drunken fans, the rivalry has not crossed the line and become ugly.

But late in Arizona State's 56–14 victory in 1996, ASU offensive lineman Glen Gable hit UA defensive lineman Daniel Greer from behind during a 95-yard interception return by the Wildcats' Mikal Smith.

The play nearly incited a riot. Gable and two other players were ejected.

"That's the most malicious thing I've ever seen," Tomey said. "Everyone was guilty, the players, the coaches, the fans, the media. It was the scariest thing I've ever been a part of."

The incident prompted Tomey and ASU coach Bruce Snyder to write a letter urging fans and players at both universities to tone down the rhetoric and the animosity. The appeals worked but make no mistake: the Civil War will never lose its intensity.

"We hate them and they hate us," ASU linebacker Derek Smith once said. "It's for real."

Terrell Suggs zeroes in on Wildcat QB Jason Johnson during the Devils' 2002 win in Tucson.

Terry Richardson's 71-yard punt return allowed Arizona State to erase a 20-5 deficit and beat Arizona 23-20 in 2005.

Mike Williams's 40 carries for 162 yards and four rushing touchdowns against Arizona in 2002 represented Pac-10 season-highs for carries and rushing scores.

The following story appeared in the 2005 edition of Athlon Sports' Pac-10 preview magazine.

DESERT DUEL

The Arizona-Arizona State Rivalry Is Heating Up

The "Duel in the Desert" is about to heat up, and the temperature gauge won't stop rising until the winner of the heated rivalry has more to play for than just bragging rights.

Arizona State's Dirk Koetter, who has taken the Sun Devils to two bowl games in four seasons, had a firm grasp on the Grand Canyon State for his first few seasons in Tempe, but times might be changing. The arrival of Mike Stoops, Arizona's fiery head coach, instantly ratcheted up the intensity of this underrated rivalry.

"There is hate, bragging rights. It makes people's seasons. It has all the ingredients of a great rivalry," Stoops says. "I like to think there has to be (more) competition to have the greatest rivalry. You have to be playing for something other than just winning the game. Hopefully, we can raise our play up to the level where that game has more significance in the Pac-10."

As of today, the Devils clearly have the upper hand. Even with Arizona's 34–27 upset last season, the Sun Devils still traveled to the Sun Bowl and knocked off Purdue while Arizona stayed at home—for the sixth straight season.

Stoops arrived at Arizona following the 2003 season with a plan to bring Wildcat football back to prominence. Before making the in-state rivalry a top priority, however, Stoops had other more pressing needs to address in Tucson. He inherited a program reeling from controversy and player revolts during the John Mackovic era. Stoops needed to work on the program's infrastructure before he worried about any opponents on the field.

It didn't take Stoops long, however, to gain the perspective he'll need against ASU, especially with the intensity growing with recruiting within the state. Koetter is already getting hot under the collar about the notion that the Wildcats are regaining control of the borders. Real hot. After the Wildcats received four early commitments last year from the top in-state players, Chaparral High School coach Ron Estabrook was quoted in The Arizona Republic saying "They're making ASU look really silly."

The numbers, however, clearly show that ASU has made it a priority to recruit in-state players. Over the past four years, the Sun Devils have signed 27 players from the State, compared to 12 from Arizona.

"I don't think this number of guys from Arizona is silly," Koetter says. "There's nobody else that has this quality or depth. If somebody else is recruiting the state of Arizona better than we are, I'd like to see who that is. We've always been committed to Arizona. There is no bigger supporter of Arizona high school football than me. That is not going to change."

The gap closed significantly this year, however, when the Wildcats signed the state's Gatorade Player of the Year, offensive lineman Daniel Borg from Tucson's Ironwood Ridge High School, as well as the two top-rated running backs, Xavier Smith of Tucson's Sunnyside High School and Terry Longbons from Centennial High School in Peoria. Another Centennial product, lineman Jordan Lowe, also signed with Arizona.

Before Stoops arrived at Arizona, Borg had "absolutely no interest" in playing for the Wildcats.

Arizona State signed four in-state products, as well—wide receiver and Phoenix Moon

A 20-5 deficit became a 23-20 Sun Devil victory in 2005.

Valley star Chris McGaha, Gilbert Highland offensive lineman Richard Tuitu'u, Phoenix Thunderbird defensive end Dexter Davis and Peoria High School tailback Keegan Herring.

"This is an area we have to cultivate and work with and do a better job," Stoops says. "When you have this much turnover and problems that we have had within our program, local players are the ones most familiar with the problems you have internally. Obviously with the change, our attitude has changed, and our perspective of the football program at the UA has hopefully changed."

So the recruiting wars have heated up in just a few short months. And with them, the intensity.

"I have no hatred for the University of Arizona. I want to beat the hell out of them, but that's not hatred," Koetter says. "That's competition."

Recently, ASU has been the superior team. The Sun Devils know it, and sometimes flaunt it.

"There's no rule in the book that says that just because it's your rival you have to play it close," Koetter said days before playing

*Andrew Carnahan stands his ground
during the 2004 renewal of the rivalry.*

Arizona last season. "If you're four touchdowns better, you can play four touchdowns better."

Not only was ASU not the better team that day, but it also lost starting quarterback Andrew Walter in the fourth quarter when the Wildcats tossed him to the ground.

Cheap shot? No. Rough play? Yes. The final outcome was an Arizona victory and possibly a change in the local perception of Wildcat football, with ESPN analysts Kirk Herbstreit and Chris Fowler noticing a possible power shift within the state.

One game—or one coach—can make a difference in an in-state rivalry like this one.

"There was a quote by Coach Koetter that the teams would show their true colors as the game wore on," Stoops said about his first win over ASU. "I think we showed our true colors. As the game wore on we kept playing more confidently and played well up until the end.... I think I have a better sense of (the rivalry), that is for sure."

Stoops knows a few things about rivalry games, having gone 6–1 against Kansas while an assistant at Kansas State and 4–1 in the "Red River Shootout" against Texas as the defensive coordinator of Oklahoma. Koetter, on the other hand, is 2–2 against Arizona since taking over in Tempe.

The Wildcats have won their share of games against ASU in the past, holding a 43–33–1 all-time series edge. But the win last season was their first in Tucson since 1998.

A 2001 victory ended with a melee on ASU's field when Wildcat players danced on the "Sparky the Sun Devil" logo on the field. Helmets were thrown, and fists were flying.

The Wildcats have done their share of dashing ASU's hopes, knocking off highly ranked Rose Bowl contenders in 1982, 1985, 1986 and 1997.

The series has gone in spurts for decades, with Arizona enjoying an 8–0–1 advantage from 1982–1990 under Larry Smith and Dick Tomey. The Wildcats put a priority on beating the Sun Devils, more so than anybody else, and at a high cost.

Smith's goals (in order) were to have fun, get an education, win the Rose Bowl and beat ASU. Privately, he probably would have put the fourth goal first. His disdain for the Sun Devils began in 1973 when he was an assistant coach with the Wildcats. That year, ASU ran up the score en route to a 55–19 victory. Smith's first Wildcat team lost 44–7 in 1980 in another one-sided affair.

Smith left town in 1986 with a five-game winning streak against the hated Sun Devils. Tomey left the program with an 8–5–1 against ASU.

Thirty years prior it was all ASU under Frank Kush.

The Sun Devils won't admit that they are looking over their shoulders now, but they understand the importance of winning the game played the day after Thanksgiving. If they forget, there's always someone there to remind them.

"There's not a day that goes by that I don't get reminded about it," Koetter says. "I was at the grocery store the other morning getting coffee and a guy walked right up to me and told me that he could not live if we couldn't go down there and beat UA. That's a lot of passion right there."

ASU VS. USC

Like most schools in the Pac-10, ASU's rivalry with USC was born out of envy.

USC has the tradition, the Pac-10 titles, the national championships, the prettiest cheerleaders. ASU, on the other hand, is still trying to make a name for itself nationally in college football, and to do that, it must go through the Trojans.

ASU's envy is also personal. The Devils recruit heavily in southern California, and many of their players were spurned by USC. They want to show the Trojans they were wrong not to offer them scholarships.

The teams didn't play each other until 1978, the year ASU and the University of Arizona joined the Pac-10. Surprisingly, ASU has held its own in the series, sporting a 9–14 mark.

But ASU hasn't beaten USC since the 1999 season, and the scores have reflected the one-sided nature of the rivalry: 48–17 in 2001, 34–13 in 2002, 37–17 in 2003, 45–7 in 2004.

ASU's 38–28 loss in 2005 was particularly frustrating. Before a standing room only crowd at Sun Devil Stadium and in near 100-degree temperatures, ASU played an inspired first half against the Matt Leinart/Reggie Bush/LenDale White-led Trojans and ran into the locker room with a 21–3 lead.

Fans were already planning ways to celebrate the end of the Trojans' 25-game winning streak.

But USC wasn't ranked No. 1 in the country on its reputation alone. It scored 35 points in the second half, and Bush and White finished with a combined 355 yards rushing and four touchdowns.

"We had them," quarterback Sam Keller said. "We just didn't finish."

There have been occasions in the rivalry when ASU did just that.

One of the greatest moments in Sun Devil history came on October 14, 1978. ASU was 4–1, its loss a humbling 51–26 trouncing at Washington State. USC, coached by John Robinson, strutted into town undefeated and with a No. 2 national ranking. It was the first meeting between the two schools.

A state-record crowd of 71,138 was in a frenzy before the game even began, and the Sun Devil players fed off the emotion.

Quarterback Mark Malone passed for 167 yards and a touchdown and ran for 139 yards and another score. But it was the ASU defense, led by defensive ends Al Harris and Ben Apuna, that was the star of the night.

Emotions in the USC series have run the gamut from frustration to elation.

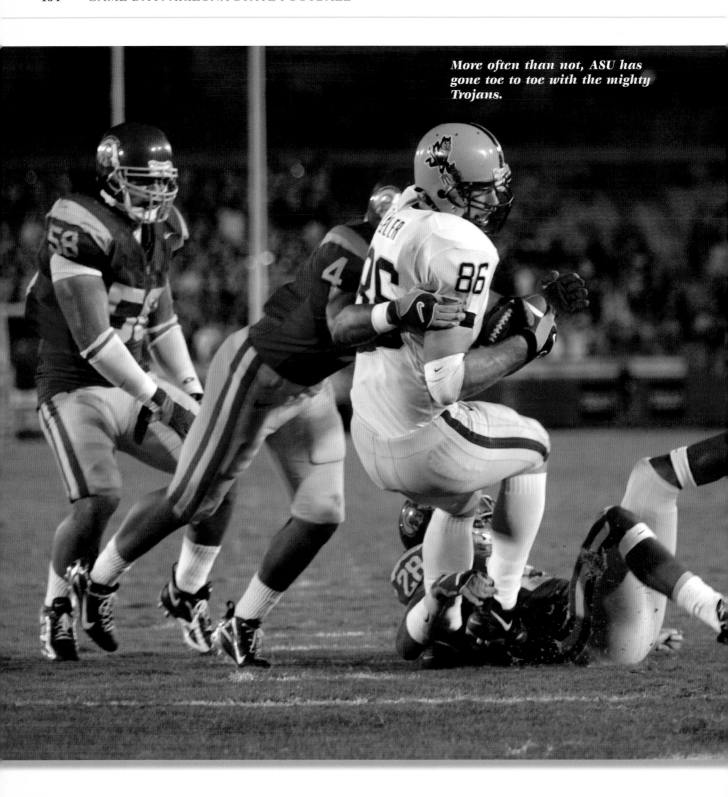

More often than not, ASU has gone toe to toe with the mighty Trojans.

The Sun Devils held All-America running back Charles White to 59 yards on 18 carries. ASU led 20–0 early in the fourth quarter, and only a late USC score averted the shutout.

Delirious Sun Devil fans stormed the field, tore down the goalposts and eventually dumped them in the Mill Avenue riverbed north of the stadium.

The Trojans would go on to beat Michigan in the Rose Bowl and share the national championship with Alabama. All 22 starters from the USC team played in the NFL.

"That game did more for our continued recognition as a potential college power," Kush said. "It said, 'We belong here.'"

Some ASU fans want to believe that USC is their natural rival because Arizona has never played in the Rose Bowl. That's more a case of wishful thinking than reality. But there's no doubt the Sun Devils circle the USC game on their calendar every year.

Most of the time, ASU turns the anticipation into disappointment.

But in October of 1996, the Sun Devils and Trojans played a classic game that defined the Rose Bowl race that season.

The 6–0 Sun Devils were ranked No. 4 in the country and had beaten No. 1 Nebraska earlier in the season. But this was still USC, and the Trojans had spanked ASU the year before, 31–0.

The Devils needed a 7-yard touchdown run from Terry Battle with 1:30 remaining to send the game into overtime.

Both teams scored touchdowns in the first overtime session. In the second overtime, Battle scored on a 25-yard run, and freshman cornerback Courtney Jackson ensured the victory when he returned a fumble 85 yards for a touchdown.

"We took USC's best punch and didn't go down," coach Bruce Snyder said. "This is a really special team. I don't know how good we really are. That won't be determined maybe until December."

The Devils were plenty good. They finished the regular season 11–0 before losing to Ohio State in the Rose Bowl.

Perhaps the strangest 60 minutes in the rivalry came in a meaningless game in 2000. Both schools were in the middle of mediocre seasons—ASU would finish 6-6 in Snyder's last year as coach—but for one night they provided some great theatre.

USC blew a 35–6 third-quarter lead before finally winning the game in double overtime, 44–38.

"I feel lousy," Snyder said.

When it comes to USC, that's an all-too-familiar feeling for the Sun Devils.

ASU VS. UCLA

The Sun Devils don't feel the same way about the Bruins as they do about the Trojans.

There's less jealousy, less animosity.

But as one of the new kids on the block in the Pac-10, ASU has had to deal with "old money" UCLA.

It's been a fairly uneventful rivalry in terms of national significance. ASU lost nine of the first 11 games as it was trying to get a foothold in the Pac-10, and in the past 10 years the Bruins haven't been the powerhouse they once were.

But there was one game that made the rivalry notable because it cemented the legend of quarterback Jake Plummer.

Again, it was 1996. This time, unlike their previous meeting, it was the Bruins in the role of spoiler, trying to knock off undefeated ASU, which was playing its first road game of the season.

But Plummer wouldn't let them.

In the fourth quarter, he threw a touchdown pass, caught a touchdown pass from freshman tailback J.R. Redmond and scored on a 1-yard quarterback sneak to erase a 28–7 lead and give ASU a 42–34 victory.

"We just put that play in this week," Snyder said of Plummer's reception. "It didn't go totally as planned, but (Plummer) went right into the teeth of the defense. It was a great run. He is so slippery. I guess that's why they call him 'The Snake.'"

ASU VS. NEBRASKA

Can eight games between schools constitute a rivalry, particularly when one school has won six of those games by a combined score of 258–111?

It can when the other two games are among the most significant victories in one school's history.

The first of ASU's two wins over Nebraska came in the 1975 Fiesta Bowl. The Sun Devils were the upstart program, still three years away from joining the Pac-10. Nebraska was, well, Nebraska.

ASU entered the game with an 11–0 record, but its wins came over Washington, Texas Christian, Brigham Young, Idaho, New Mexico, Colorado State, UTEP, Utah, Wyoming, Pacific and Arizona.

Not exactly Murderer's Row.

Few people outside the Sun Devils' locker room gave ASU much of a chance. But coach Frank Kush knew better. He had a spectacular wide receiver in John Jefferson and an All-America cornerback in Mike Haynes.

Plus, the game was being played in Sun Devil Stadium, giving ASU an enormous home field advantage.

The Sun Devils kept the Cornhuskers at bay for most of the game, then won on a late field goal by Danny Kush, the coach's son.

The win put ASU on the college football map.

"Everybody knows who we are now," Kush said.

Twenty-one years later, ASU again faced its skeptics.

In 1995, the Sun Devils traveled to Lincoln to play the Cornhuskers. Safety Mitchell Freedman ran onto the field carrying a banner that said, "Bring the Pain."

Nebraska did, winning 77–28.

The Devils, who thought Nebraska needlessly ran up the score, fumed for an entire year. The revenge, though, was worth the anguish.

Nebraska came to Tempe in September of 1996 ranked No. 1 in the country. It was early in the Sun Devils' Rose Bowl season, so no one knew how good ASU actually was.

After the game, everyone did.

ASU dominated Nebraska, shutting down the Cornhuskers' vaunted running game to win 19–0.

Because the Sun Devils were a Pac-10 fixture by that time, it wasn't as historically significant as the 1975 game. But perhaps ASU wouldn't have gotten to Pasadena without the confidence it carried forward from that night.

"I knew we were going to win," defensive tackle Shawn Swayda said. "Everybody else had their doubts, but we never did. I am totally tired but it's the best feeling I've ever had."

Talkin' Arizona State Football

Why should we talk about the tradition, history and allure of the Sun Devils when some former players and coaches do it so well?

"Dude, I'm not planning on staying that long. *I've got things to do."*

—PAT TILLMAN, LB, 1994–1997,
WHEN COACH BRUCE SNYDER ASKED HIM ABOUT REDSHIRTING

"One of the great things *about going to ASU was the almost always sunny days. I enjoyed the walks from the dorm to my classes and the number of opportunities to study outside under a shady tree with a tall cup of ice tea. While walking to class, for fun I would sometimes use the time to visualize myself following my blockers and deciding when to accelerate or slow down as if returning a punt, a kick or an interception. The weather provided plenty of good opportunities for that."*

—MIKE HAYNES, CB, 1972–1975

"I came to Arizona State on a football scholarship, and I shall always be indebted to Frank Kush for instilling toughness in his players. He was as tough as Charles Finley and George Steinbrenner rolled into one."

—REGGIE JACKSON, 1965

"Frank Kush was able to get something out of me that no one else could get. He affected hundreds of athletes that he coached in that same way."

—DANNY WHITE, QB, 1971–1973

"I think if I told them we were walking to the Bay Area, they wouldn't ask why. They'd just do it."

—BRUCE SNYDER ON THE 1996 ASU TEAM THAT FINISHED 11–1
AND CAME WITHIN 100 SECONDS OF A NATIONAL CHAMPIONSHIP

"I'm proud to say that I was a part of the 1996 Pac-10 champions. That was the most fun I had during my entire playing career. I remember the great fans and the great crowds. When we played UCLA in the Rose Bowl during the regular season I told my teammates to turn around on the bus and look at the stadium one more time because we were going to be back there in January. I will always cherish my Arizona State memories."

—JAKE PLUMMER, QB, 1993–1996

Jake Plummer

Andrew Walter

"He'd come to my office *at 10 or 11* PM *every night. We'd sit down and talk about God or Kosovo or poor people in this country. He wanted me to read the Book of Mormon. So we did."*

—FORMER ASU LINEBACKERS COACH LYLE SETENCICH ON PAT TILLMAN

"Being a Sun Devil athlete *is something that lasts much longer than four or five years; it's a lifetime membership to an elite fraternity of friends, tradition, and pride."*

—NICK MURPHY, P, 1999–2001

"There is not a single player in college football *who means more to his team than Jake Plummer. We all should just be enjoying this guy, not just at Arizona State. He's a heck of a football player. He is one of the best young players I have ever been around. If I were starting a team from scratch, he would be my first pick."*

—COACH BRUCE SNYDER BEFORE 1997 ROSE BOWL AGAINST OHIO STATE

"Before the Nebraska game, *we had a team meeting, players only. That was the first time … I saw Pat speak out. I think we broke a grease-board and some chairs."*

—RICKY BOYER, WR, 1995–1997

"Tempe is a great town with great fans. *Knowing what I know now, I would not have gone to school anywhere else."*

—ANDREW WALTER, QB, 2001–2004

*"**Dirk Koetter is one of the best coaches** I have ever learned from. Not only did he teach me the game of football, but he also taught me the game of life. He developed me into a complete player and a complete person."*

—TERRELL SUGGS, DE, 2000–2002

*"**The first three years that I was a head coach,** Frank Kush was a loyal, hard-working and intelligent assistant coach to me at Arizona State. Without his dedication and help, we never would have had the outstanding record that we had during those years. He was named my successor at the age of 29, and his record over the next two decades speaks for itself."*

—DAN DEVINE, COACH, 1955–1957

*"**I am very very fortunate** to have been educated at Arizona State University. Not only was I prepped for success in the real world, but having played football for the Sun Devils has provided countless opportunities. ASU has the finest weather, facilities and student body in college football. Our rich tradition made my playing experience second to none and I continue to follow the football program closely in its successes."*

—SCOTT PETERS, C, 1998–2001

"Today, we lost a truly great young man; *very simply, the ultimate American. To me, Pat Tillman is, without question, the biggest 'hero' of my lifetime. During my tenure at ASU, Pat was often referred to—by many of us—as 'Braveheart.' How incredibly ironic, years later, that Pat will go down in the annals of American history as the quintessential, in every way, braveheart."*

—ATHLETIC DIRECTOR KEVIN WHITE, 1996–2000

"There was a saying at the time *that if you could play for Coach Frank Kush you could play for anybody. You do not know how true that was. You had to be there to see it and witness what I'm talking about. The man had a job to do, take young boys and make them into men. Men that would be able to give 150 percent on the football field and the same off the field towards your education."*

—BRENT McCLANAHAN, RB, 1970–1972

"I'm not the kind of person *to stand up and say, 'Look at me, I'm Jake Plummer.' If I would have done that when I was younger, my older brothers (Brett, 27, and Eric, 25) would have socked me in the arm, knocked me over and put me right down to the level I should be."*

—JAKE PLUMMER, QB, 1993–1996

*"**The best days of my life** were when I was a student-athlete at ASU. Donning the Maroon and Gold on Saturdays and playing alongside my Sun Devil brothers was special and I take great pride in what we accomplished as a team and I cherish the relationships I have with my brothers to this day. Athletics is just part of the experience though. ASU is full of great people who do a great job in supporting student-athletes. Everyone I met on campus—whether it be professors, academic advisors, or the staff at the scholarship office—made my days as a college student great. The Athletic Department staff also provided tremendous support and always had the best interests of the athletes in mind. ASU is about family; once you're in, you're in for life!"*

—JUAN ROQUE, OL, 1994–1996

*"**I wasn't necessarily blessed** with a tremendous amount of athletic ability. But what I lacked in ability, I made up for in determination. And I probably played for the right kind of guy when it came to that, because Frank (Kush) was obviously a disciplinarian. He knew exactly what he wanted out of you."*

—JIM KANE, OL, 1966–1968

*"**He couldn't hit a bull** in the butt with a handful of popcorn."*

—FRANK KUSH AFTER HIS FIELD GOAL KICKER MISSED A POTENTIAL GAME-WINNING KICK

Juan Roque

John Cooper

"This is the biggest dang victory *I've ever been associated with! I don't want to sit down. I'm on cloud nine!"*

—COACH JOHN COOPER ON 1987 ROSE BOWL VICTORY OVER MICHIGAN

"As a child, I grew up watching Sun Devil athletics *with my dad. I eventually had the opportunity to play for ASU. I'm excited to take my own kids to watch the Sun Devils play and instill in them love for the Maroon and Gold just like my dad did with me when I was younger."*

—PAUL REYNOLDS, S, 1996–1997

"I knew we were going to win. *Everybody else had their doubts, but we never did. I am totally tired but it's the best feeling I've ever had."*

—SHAWN SWAYDA, DT, 1993–1996, AFTER ASU'S
19–0 VICTORY OVER NO. 1 NEBRASKA IN 1996

"It's difficult to describe my feelings. *I'm so happy. We beat our archrival at their place and we're going to the Rose Bowl undefeated. I'm going to vote us No. 1. I've not seen a better team."*

—COACH BRUCE SNYDER AFTER ASU BEAT ARIZONA 56–14
IN 1996 TO FINISH THE REGULAR SEASON 11–0

Traditions and Pageantry

Arizona State boasted consistent success under Hall of Fame coaches Dan Devine and Frank Kush in the Western Athletic Conference. That level of play has been difficult to replicate since the school joined the Pac-10 in 1978, though ASU does have two Rose Bowl appearances to its credit.

The challenge of playing in one of the best conferences in college football hasn't prevented ASU from maintaining and enhancing some of college football's greatest traditions. Here's a sampling of what makes Arizona State football unique.

THE SUN DEVILS

The current nickname is the third in the school's history. When the football program was born at then-Tempe Normal School in 1889, the team was called the Owls. The Bulldogs was the second nickname, after the school became known as Arizona State Teachers' College.

It's unclear when the Sun Devil idea was hatched, but a series of articles in the *State Press*, the campus newspaper, in 1946 urged the school to adopt the new mascot. On November 8, 1946, the student body overwhelmingly approved the name change in a special election.

Now that ASU had a new mascot, someone had to design it. The man commissioned was Bert Anthony, an artist for Walt Disney. He designed a Sun Devil and named him "Sparky." Does the fact that Sparky was designed by a Disney artist make him a distant cousin of Mickey Mouse?

Interestingly, a sun devil, if taken literally, is in no way demonic. According to ASU's School of Climatology, a "sun devil" is similar to a dust devil, where unusual atmospheric conditions are caused by a high amount of sunlight. Since no one has yet to come up with a clever logo for atmospheric conditions to put on the side of a football helmet, ASU is wise to stick with Sparky.

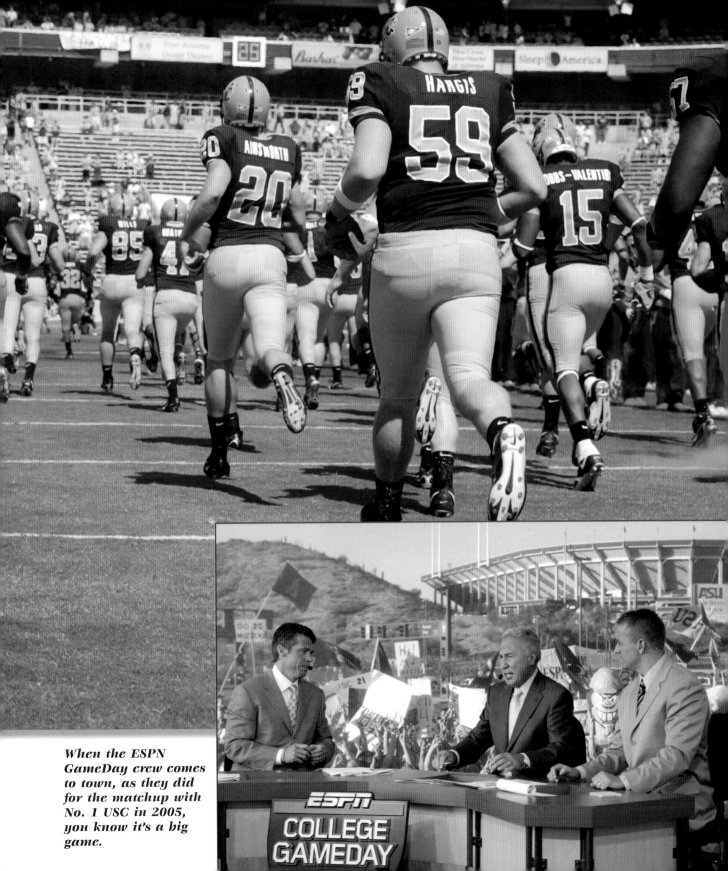

When the ESPN
GameDay crew comes
to town, as they did
for the matchup with
No. 1 USC in 2005,
you know it's a big
game.

ASU FIGHT SONG

Fight, Devils down the field

Fight with your might and don't ever yield

Long may our colors outshine all others

Echo from the buttes, give 'em hell Devils!

Cheer, Cheer for ASU

Fight for the old Maroon

For it's Hail, Hail, The Gang's All Here

And it's onward to victory!

ALMA MATER

Where the bold saguaros

Raise their arms on high

Praying strength for brave tomorrows

From the western sky

Where eternal mountains

Kneel at sunset's gate

Here we hail thee, Alma Mater

Arizona State

CAMPUS LANDMARKS

Sun Devil Stadium

ASU's home field doesn't boast the number of skyboxes and other revenue-raising amenties of some of college football's palaces. A high upper-deck seat results in quite a hike, and the wait for the restrooms can sometimes be an adventure. Big deal. Situated between two buttes, the structure remains one of the more visually impressive in college football, and the atmosphere when the stadium is full can be downright raucous.

Constructed in 1958, the stadium boasted only one deck until the mid-1970s. Prompted by the growth of ASU, the Phoenix area and the Fiesta Bowl—which called the facility home from 1971–2006—Sun Devil Stadium grew to nearly 80,000 seats.

ASU likes to call Sun Devil Stadium the "House of Heat" because of the pressure-cooker atmosphere it hopes visiting teams experience. During early-season games scheduled in the afternoon for television, the facility earns that name, but for a different and much more literal reason. The temperature at kickoff for September and October afternoon games can reach triple digits, testing the players' endurance and potentially altering the coaches' strategy.

The school's sports information department does not compile a list of its all-time warmest games because it does not want to publicly release information that could be viewed as a liability in recruiting.

But how much has ASU really been at an advantage in the heat? Consider that in four recent September-October hot-weather games, the Sun Devils routed Stanford but lost twice to USC and were drilled by Oregon.

As the saying goes, both teams have to play in it.

"It's definitely a factor, but since we are in it all the time, it's something that you can embrace and take it on your side," said Kyle Caldwell, a defensive end at ASU from 2003 to 2006. "But it's in the minds of all the players on both teams. It's a matter of who is more mentally tough."

Palm Walk

A popular campus corridor for students and skateboarders, Palm Walk—named for the palm trees that line both sides—runs from the dormitories north of University Drive to the Memorial Union hall at the center of campus.

The trees were the brainchild of Normal School president Arthur John Matthews, who envisioned an "evergreen" campus—at least as much as was possible in a desert setting. His vision became reality, as today the ASU campus is a nationally recognized arboretum.

In case you find yourself on Palm Walk at ASU, we'll save you the trouble of counting the trees. There are 111 of them.

Gammage Auditorium

Approach the campus from the south on Mill Avenue, and Gammage Auditorium will be the first thing to catch your eye. Designed by famed architect Frank Lloyd Wright—in fact, the structure is considered his last commission—it opened in 1964 and was christened with a performance by the Philadelphia Orchestra.

The auditorium, which seats 3,017, is the site of plays, musicals, concerts, lectures and—in 2004—the third presidential debate between George W. Bush and John Kerry.

Tempe Butte/"A" Mountain

The butte to the west of the stadium is home to one of the ASU community's most enduring landmarks: a large concrete "A" that can be seen from miles to the south. Most of the time, the letter is painted gold, but the colors sometimes change before the annual game against the University of Arizona.

Wildcats supporters, in the dark of night, aim to repaint the letter red and blue—Arizona's colors—in the days before the Territorial Cup game. They have often been successful, despite attempts by ASU students to protect the letter.

One would think that ASU students wouldn't need to provide much security, considering the headquarters of the Tempe Police Department sits at the bottom of "A" Mountain. Rumor has it, though, that the Tempe police do not mind being a little, uh, lax in checking the butte on the nights before the big game, since a few in the department are Arizona graduates.

Give the Arizona vandals credit though—considering that it takes about 150 gallons of paint to cover the "A," vandalizing their archrival's landmark does not come cheap.

Mill Avenue

No, this isn't actually a part of the ASU campus. But no discussion of college life in Tempe would be complete without mention of the intimate-yet-vibrant strip of shops, restaurants and bars often mentioned as one of the best hangout spots, well, anywhere.

Mill Avenue was once inhabited primarily by local mom-and-pop shops, but it has since gone corporate, with most of the establishments today being of the chain variety. Still, there is charm, and walking up and down the street and people-watching on a Friday or Saturday night makes for a nice, inexpensive evening.

CAMP TONTOZONA

This is another landmark that is actually not on campus, but ASU owns the land in the Tonto forest about 100 miles northeast of Tempe, where the football team has conducted preseason workouts since 1960. Legendary coach Frank Kush hatched the idea as a way to get the Sun Devils out of the blistering August heat of the Valley of the Sun.

During his tenure as Sun Devil coach from 1980 to 1984, Darryl Rogers was known to, on occasion, let his assistants finish practice, grab a fishing pole, and relax alongside clear-running Tonto Creek.

However, Tontozona's most infamous physical feature is the steep hill beyond the practice field, which Kush often commanded his players to climb—as a conditioning drill, as punishment for a team rules violation, or simply because he felt like it. The hill has been dubbed "Mount Kush."

MASCOT

If you're an ASU student interested in dressing up in the Sparky Sun Devil suit to entertain the crowd at a football game, it would behoove you to be as physically fit as the guys on the field. For starters, early-season contests can be steamy—even more so for individuals who happen to be attending the game in a mascot suit.

Indeed, it was an ASU gymnast, Dick Jacobs, who was the first to don the Sparky suit at a football game. The identities of the students who personify Sparky have been kept top-secret, but one can safely bet the mortgage that more than a few gymnasts have had that duty since Jacobs.

After all, game day isn't limited to standing on the sidelines, holding a pitchfork and chatting with the cheerleaders—no, this is work. Sparky is required to be athletic, often being called on to perform an array of jumps and flips. And some buffness in the biceps and chest is recommended, because after every score, Sparky is required to do one push-up for every point that the Sun Devils have amassed.

TAILGATING

As a commuter campus in a metropolitan area, ASU doesn't have the same tailgating tradition as, say, a Penn State, where the RVs start rolling into State College on Friday afternoon. Sure, there are some fans doing their pregame partaking in the parking lot, but many opt for the air-conditioned comfort of one of the many bars and restaurants within walking distance of Sun Devil Stadium in downtown Tempe.

Unfortunately, the extracurricular entertainment options of Sun Devil faithful took a huge hit in 2006 when McDuffy's, one of the top sports bars in the country, closed its doors.

Rudy Carpenter

Facts and Figures

CAREER STATISTICAL LEADERS

- Rushes: 675, Woody Green, 1971–1973
- Rushing yards: 4,188, Woody Green, 1971–1973
- Passing attempts: 1,416, Andrew Walter, 2001–2004
- Completions: 777, Andrew Walter, 2001–2004
- Passing yardage: 10,617, Andrew Walter, 2001–2004
- Completion percentage: Rudy Carpenter, 62.4, 2005–present
- Touchdown passes: 85, Andrew Walter, 2001–2004
- Receptions: 258, Derek Hagan, 2002–2005
- Receiving yardage: 3,939, Derek Hagan, 2002–2005
- Receiving touchdowns: 27, Derek Hagan, 2002–2005
- Total offense: 10,142, Andrew Walter, 2001–2004
- Punt return average: 17.7, Wilford White, 1947–1950
- Kickoff return average: 28.3, Wilford White, 1947–1950
- All-purpose yardage: 5,654, Wilford White, 1947–1950
- Punting average: 44.9, Stephen Baker, 1998–1999
- Scoring: 380, Luis Zendejas, 1981–1984
- Interceptions: 18, Mike Richardson, 1979–1982
- Tackles: 425, Greg Battle, 1982–1985
- Sacks: 44, Terrell Suggs, 2000–2002
- Tackles for loss: 65.5, Terrell Suggs, 2000–2002

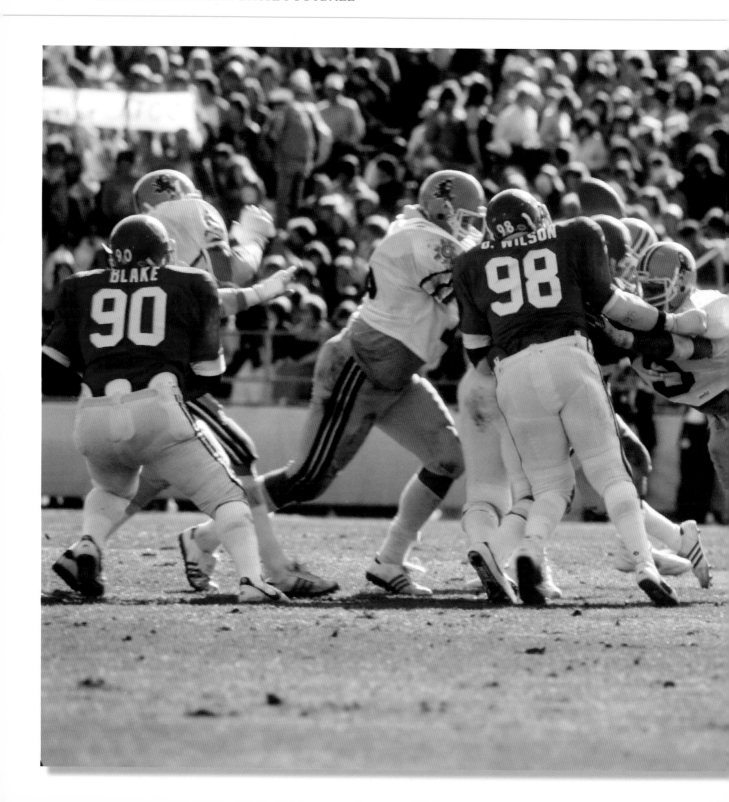

ALL-TIME BOWL GAME SCORES

BOWL	DATE	SCORE
Sun	January 1, 1940	Arizona State 0, Catholic University 0
Sun	January 1, 1941	Case Western Reserve 26, Arizona State 13
Salad	January 2, 1950	Xavier 33, Arizona State 21
Salad	January 1, 1951	Miami (Ohio) 34, Arizona State 21
Peach	December 30, 1970	Arizona State 48, North Carolina 26
Fiesta	December 27, 1971	Arizona State 45, Florida State 38
Fiesta	December 23, 1972	Arizona State 49, Missouri 35
Fiesta	December 21, 1973	Arizona State 28, Pittsburgh 7
Fiesta	December 26, 1975	Arizona State 17, Nebraska 14
Fiesta	December 25, 1977	Penn State 42, Arizona State 30
Garden State	December 16, 1978	Arizona State 34, Rutgers 18
Fiesta	January 1, 1983	Arizona State 32, Oklahoma 21
Holiday	December 22, 1985	Arkansas 18, Arizona State 17
Rose	January 1, 1987	Arizona State 22, Michigan 15
Freedom	December 30, 1987	Arizona State 33, Air Force 28
Rose	January 1, 1997	Ohio State 20, Arizona State 17
Sun	December 31, 1997	Arizona State 17, Iowa 7
Aloha	December 25, 1999	Wake Forest 23, Arizona State 3
Aloha	December 25, 2000	Boston College 31, Arizona State 17
Holiday	December 27, 2002	Kansas State 34, Arizona State 27
Sun	December 21, 2004	Arizona State 27, Purdue 23
Insight	December 27, 2005	Arizona State 45, Rutgers 40
Hawaii	December 24, 2006	Hawaii 41, Arizona State 24

Overall

Won 12, Lost 10, Tied 1

1983 Fiesta Bowl

Terrell Suggs

SUN DEVILS IN THE COLLEGE FOOTBALL HALL OF FAME

Name	Position	Years	Inducted
Dan Devine	Coach	1955–1957	1985
Mike Haynes	Cornerback	1972–1975	2001
John Jefferson	Wide receiver	1974–1977	2002
Frank Kush	Coach	1958–1979	1995
Ron Pritchard	Linebacker	1966–1968	2003
Danny White	Quarterback	1970–1973	1998

CONSENSUS ALL-AMERICANS

2002	Terrell Suggs
1996	Juan Roque
1987	Randall McDaniel
1986	Danny Villa
1985	David Fulcher
1984	David Fulcher
1983	Luis Zendejas
1982	Mike Richardson
1981	Mike Richardson
1978	Al Harris
1977	John Jefferson
1975	Mike Haynes
1973	Woody Green
1972	Woody Green
1968	Ron Pritchard

SUN DEVILS IN THE PRO FOOTBALL HALL OF FAME

Charley Taylor, RB/WR
Inducted: 1984
Arizona State: 1961–1963
Washington Redskins, 1964-77
- NFL Rookie of the Year in 1964
- Led NFL in receiving 1966, 1967
- Played in eight Pro Bowls
- 649 catches for 9,110 yards, 79 TDs

John Henry Johnson, RB
Inducted: 1987
Arizona State: 1952
San Francisco 49ers, 1954–1956
Detroit Lions, 1957–1959
Pittsburgh Steelers, 1960–1965
Houston Oilers, 1966
- Named to four Pro Bowls
- First Steeler to rush for 1,000 yards
- 6,803 rushing yards